~~~~~~~~~~~~~~~~~~~

HOME FRO...
CONTENT...

'Roxy Beaujolais is the woman behind the bar men fantasise about. She can also assume a good deal of the responsibility for the revival of the pub as a tempting and satisfying place to eat.' (Fay Maschler, restaurant and food-in-pubs critic of the *Evening Standard*)

'Roxy Beaujolais, a name to conjure with, casts spells in her Soho kitchen where she makes magic for the customers of The Three Greyhounds. Her recipes lift pub grub to new rarefied heights. I wish that she took prisoners.' (Jeffrey Bernard)

Jenny Hoffmann Silver is an Australian who has lived in London since 1973. After several years running the front-of-house at Ronnie Scott's in Soho she became chef in the Green Room for the Royal Shakespeare Company at the Barbican, then went on to run her own private catering business, trading under the name 'Roxy Beaujolais'. Since 1985 she has been a publican and restaurant manager. From her flagships *The Three Greyhounds* and the *Soho Brasserie* in the heart of the West End, Roxy has been at the forefront of pub food for the last fifteen years. Perhaps because she was born in Australia, she has a unique understanding of good British pub-keeping – one that has won her a faithful crowd of regulars all over London.

HOME FROM THE INN CONTENTED

A cookbook of simple, popular pub food

Roxy Beaujolais

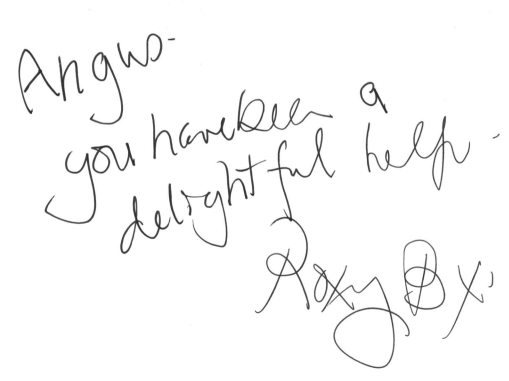

Angus —
you have been a
delightful help —
Roxy B x

KYLE CATHIE LIMITED

~~~~~~

My husband, Nathan Silver, has helped with everything. Considering where both our primary gastronomic learning experiences were obtained, it seems no less than just that this book should be dedicated to our mothers. So here's to:

Clare Carmody Hoffmann and Libby Nachimowsky Silver

– Roxy Beaujolais, London 1995

First published in Great Britain in 1996 by
Kyle Cathie Limited
20 Vauxhall Bridge Road
London SW1V 2SA

ISBN 1 85526 213 8

Text © 1996 Auricula Press Inc.
Photography © 1996 James Mortimer
Illustrations © 1949 Estate of Edward Ardizzone

Roxy Beaujolais is hereby identified as the author of this work in accordance with Section 77 of the Copyright, Designs and Patents Act 1988.

A CIP catalogue record for this title is available from the British Library.

Typeset by SX Composing DTP
Printed and bound in Spain by GraphyCems.

Cover photo:
Roxy Beaujolais in her home kitchen, showing (left to right in rows from rear to front of table):Potato Bread, page 16; grapes; Moules Soho, page 95; A Stiff One cocktail, page 140; Sydney Opera House Salad, page 44; Gilded Pheasants, page 83; Spicy Italian Sausages with Pesto Sauce and Tagliatelle, page 50; a pint of Adnams Best real ale; Cremona mustard, a chutney of candied fruits, page 28; Spiced Ox Tongue with Broad Beans, page 28; Melbourne Mowbray Pie, page 38; Mamabel's Tortilla, page 111

CONTENTS

ACKNOWLEDGEMENTS

T S Eliot makes the point that true novelty is hardly possible in poetry, and when it occurs, it's unsatisfactory – a good poet just achieves the Next Thing. In other words, the poet must stand on the shoulders of those who have gone before, since something really novel would probably be incomprehensible.

Sounds right for my job, too.

My own very mildly creative occupation, cooking in pubs, is completely about dealing with the familiar. So much so that its main danger isn't some trendy change for change's sake, it's overpredictability. I dice with banality. And I know that avoiding the insipid can be as tough as avoiding unnecessary novelty.

Which is why I'm certain that writing to explain a better way of making a potato salad, or of cooking a plate of corned beef – that is, explaining how to prepare the simplest of foods satisfyingly – has been worthwhile. Of course it's highly dependent on the people being cooked for: my guests. Their tastes always determine what is the best Present Thing, as well as the best Next Thing.

And certainly it depends on others whose shoulders I stand on, explainers before me. In this book, when I've knowingly relied on someone else's fine food idea, I've acknowledged my source. A thousand apologies where I've unintentionally omitted a credit if it has happened. (Though in Eliot's terms, reliances continually happen, and borrowings go on forever.)

For the loan of serving china and napery used in some photographs, I am very grateful to Thomas Goode and Co., the Wedgewood Hotel and Restaurant Division, and Natalie Gibson.

INTRODUCTION

Whom this book is for

After some consideration, I have decided to write about innkeeper's food and British pubs as if you came of drinking age in Samoa, caught a plane and arrived in London. That is because this book might well be profitably consulted by readers who have never been to a British inn. And also because even some of my English acquaintances – let alone the Australians and Americans – appear to know nothing about pubs, pub society and pub food. For these deserving cultural travellers, a semi-ethnographic approach and a bit of discussion seem appropriate.

Most readers may wish to consult this book for more particular motives: because they know and love pubs, or are considering catering for the fantasy of friends or relatives who know and love pubs; or because they think pubs, therefore pub food, appeal to men (actually pubs only appeal to some of them); or because they suppose an innkeeper's food is worth a look since it must be pretty straightforward and easy to do (this much is true). I mean to satisfy their desires, too. If I had to put my subject in a sentence, this book is about how to cook simply for guests. Obviously, customers as well as innkeepers often need to do it.

The food of inns

The last decent book about pubs was written in 1949.[1] It described an institution entirely devoted to conviviality and the sale of drink, and it mentioned food only in connection with the servings of nine London pubs. Why so few? Listen, Samoan, and I will offer my own perception.

---

1 Maurice Gorham's *Back to the Local*; a sequel to his prewar book *The Local*, bringing his story of English pubs up to the midcentury. In my opinion, this slim volume (beautifully illustrated by Edward Ardizzone) is terrific. A short bibliography of other books on English pubs is on page 141.

In early history, inns were places for travellers to eat, drink, feed horses and sleep. So it was for a long time. But by the late 19th century, hotels and restaurants had come into existence, taking over the sleeping and eating functions. In Britain the breweries began to buy up inns in order to assure ongoing sales. The popular drink in Britain was beer, so British pubs became their fountains.

As a result of the inn's changing place in society and commerce, innkeeper's food declined, and some time before the First World War disappeared from notice. Perhaps the long period that followed was really the golden age of pubs, when they were exclusively concerned with drink and conviviality. At least that is how it has been frequently described in fiction, and more factually by thoughtful observers since the 1920s.[2]

Then in the early 1970s, something happened: food began to feature again in British inns. My considered explanation is that the food operation (as the managing breweries call it) began to be noticed as a worthwhile source of income just about the time that serious drinking, particularly by louts in groups, started to become conspicuously objectionable.

In 1989 came the Conservative government's Beer Orders legislation, aimed at increasing consumer choice by forcing the big breweries to sell and lease off the 'tied' pubs. The effect was largely the reverse. Many ties remained or were newly established because of the property sales, and beer price increases since 1989 have gone at twice the rate of inflation. The main bit of good news was that because of rising profits, the industry began redefining itself. New, efficient, retail-savvy pub groups began to emerge like J D Wetherspoon, Tom Cobleigh, Yates Brothers, Regent Inns and Grosvenor Inns. They bought up some existing pubs, but many of their places were converted from banks, showrooms, dry cleaners or other commercial property that could win planning and licensing approvals. Easily accessible toilets for the disabled was a way these new pub groups had of winning licensing magistrates' hearts, one brewer told me.

The new pub properties don't necessarily have *prominent* frontage (sometimes, champion pubs are a bit hidden), but they have strong locations, positions, or exterior personalities that are

---

2 For a contemporaneous survey, see Ernest Selley's 1927 book, *The English Public House As It Is.*

exploited well in design. They almost always include space for outdoor tables, because Britain is becoming much more sidewalk-café-minded. And of course, they feature food as well as drink. Not because low-cost food in itself is hugely profitable, but because it's what the customers want – and they stay to drink.

The savvy pubs serve food like this: customers order over the bar, pay for their food as they order, and find a seat unless they prefer to drink and eat off a ledge. When the order is ready, the bartender calls the customer back to the bar, or delivers the food to the table if he/she knows where the customer is. At some of the larger new pubs each table has a brass plaque with a number, and the customer tells the bartender what number table he's at so the staff can find him.

The problems

Some well-behaved, not entirely hidebound drinkers in convivial British pubs still deplore the earnest spread of pub food, and from the other side of the bar I sympathise with them a little. Diners get in the way of drinkers in the public house. They are often in the Public Bar, or indeed (nowadays) in the one and only bar available to all. On the other hand, from the opposing point of view of the seated diner, standing drinkers' elbows and mugs and bottoms get in the way. The necessity of selling both drink and food in one small space is a real problem for everyone. A separate dining room is an obvious answer, but then a pub becomes something else: a restaurant and bar.

Another thing is that food smells. The smells are often stronger than wafts of tobacco and beer and urinals, which is very off-putting when it comes from the horrible kind of pub food redolent of frying, onions, recycled leftovers and dried-up meat pies. But to counter that, I know fresh, imaginative food can have a come-hither call to drinkers. It's pleasant to catch a whiff of a sweet-cured herring on a piece of warm onion bread, a char-grilled lamb cutlet, or the landlady's own special meat pie. On balance, I'm sure that palatable food can almost always be achieved within the narrow functional confines of a pub.

About me

The new shape of booze retailing was at first a distant trumpet, then a wake-up call for me. I'd come to Britain from Australia in

1973, and over the years had moved inexorably towards committed innkeeping. After several years running the front-of-house at Ronnie Scott's in Soho, I cooked in the Green Room at the Barbican for the Royal Shakespeare Company actors and crew, then I went on to run my own private catering business, trading under the name Roxy Beaujolais (as I still do).

In 1985 I became a publican and restaurant manager for the J & W Nicholson division of Allied Domecq plc. I started by running The Unicorn in St James's (where I was cited by Fay Maschler in London's *Evening Standard* for helping to pioneer pub food excellence), then I managed The Soho Brasserie in Old Compton Street in Soho. After 18 months I moved a few metres further east to The Three Greyhounds at the corner of Old Compton and Greek Streets, taking over a previous tenancy as Nicholson's publican and manager.

Overall, my efforts have been appreciated. The major pub guidebooks by Angus McGill of *The Evening Standard* and *Time Out* were very kind in both 1995 and 1996. The public has turned up in growing numbers – often they're locals; frequently they're from the USA, France or Sweden because they've seen a guidebook. I'm determined to hold my name-dropping to the absolute minimum necessary for verisimilitude, but I'm proud that Sir Isaiah Berlin and Sir Stephen Spender sometimes ate with me as dining members of the Cranium Club, that Julian Clary often popped in, and that Jeffrey Bernard, London's most famous drinker, mentions me in his *Spectator* columns, alongside my neighbouring colleague Norman Balon at the Coach and Horses.

Pub food's popularity

Taking my cards off the table and getting back down to the issue, why should anyone be enthusiastic about pub food? It seems to me that food prepared by others is always a sort of journey, but usually – let's face it – we favour a gastronomic trip just down to the corner rather than to the limits of imagination. It generally suits us to stay within the local map of conviviality, tastes and tradition, and plainly, good pub food in Britain (like good bistro food in France) is the centre of our gastronomic tradition. Why? No doubt because it's distinct, unfussy, flavourful, comforting. It's also low-cost, quick to arrive, served in a great atmosphere, and – perhaps this is the clincher – it's accompanied by one or more relaxing drinks that need no justification when guzzled in context. No wonder pub food stays popular. It's even becoming healthier. Increasingly, some of the best new places to eat are pubs.

Pub food quality

So, can the food in British pubs really be good? Complaints still abound, often combined with prejudices. One pub guidebook published not long ago sneers that 'managed pubs' in towns and cities feature standardised menus, and 'what passes as "cooking" is generally the outcome of an unholy alliance between the freezer and the microwave'. It thinks that 'home cooking' is more likely at those dear country pubs that devotedly display 'an honest approach based on fresh ingredients'. And 'if there is a talented cook on the premises (it might even be the licensee)', the guidebook patronises,

> ... some fruitful cottage economy might also show up in the form of home-smoked fish, hand-made sausages or home-baked bread. This is exactly the kind of food that a good country pub should tackle, in preference to yet another round of Continental clichés.[3]

As a London publican who has smoked many a fish and baked many a loaf, I know that such comments are precious rubbish. Cities have wonderful sources for meat, smoked fish and bread, and not just in Soho where I mainly buy. One can find a chunky Toulouse or peppery Italian sausage in many decent urban butchers, if those things strike you (as they do me) as Continental achievements rather than clichés. In my view – and I speak as a leader in modernising pub food, for what it's worth – good pub food doesn't require 100 percent home cooking. It requires simplicity, good taste (which includes good *taste*) and a broad sense of rightness.

The now very large number of customers who eat in pubs do so because they like the low cost, the speed, the atmosphere and having an easy-to-order drink with their food. They say pub food at its best *is* wonderful, which is accurate comment if one acknowledges two scales of judgement: the convenience/cost

---

3 *Which? Guide to Country Pubs*, London 1993.

scale and the absolute quality scale. But I wouldn't dodge the quest for absolute quality either. And no doubt there is a substantial gap in the market between the ordinary and the best. My brief is to take up these challenges, accept the limitations of convenience/cost and show how the ordinary can be made into the beguiling.

My mission statement

So what sort of cooking am I advocating in this book? Refined simplicity without perfectionism. The chef Rick Stein argues that the genius of English food is its simplicity, and he thinks English cooking often tastes terrible because simplicity is so dependent upon perfect materials and precise methods.[4] His observation is astute and true as far as it goes, which is to the point of diminishing returns: when you become afraid to even make an attempt because you might violate high principle. The best becomes the enemy of the good when fears are fanned by counterproductive foodie extremism, such as I have found in another recent English cookbook that relentlessly takes readers to task about ultra-freshness and ultra-extra-ness in everything – I won't name the book. Perfection is an unarguable aim, but to browbeat readers about it is presumptuous and boring, and the patronising intimation that we are probably unworthy is downright provoking (ultra-extra, huh? Nuke the whales!).

I'm certainly prepared to admit that ultra-fresh free range eggs are strongly advisable for sunny side ups or perfect truffled scrambled eggs, but to the person withstanding the heat in the kitchen it's usually more relevant to know that for glazing a pie, a stale ordinary egg may do. Cooks have a right to be *quite good enough* whenever perfectionism becomes an obstacle. My code of practice is to only specify (for example) home-made stock when the recipe at issue requires my advising that it's greatly preferable in the circumstances to a stock cube. And I suggest merely using commercial mayonnaise whisked with puréed garlic for beef sandwiches, because it's quick and absolutely good enough for that particular purpose. And, read on: I sometimes even unashamedly uphold the virtues of those sovereign bottled preparations, Tabasco, Worcestershire sauce and Maggi seasoning. I'm

---

4 In his *Taste of the Sea*, London 1995.

all for frozen oysters and ready-puréed garlic.

Making these terrible compromises could explain why I cook in pubs instead of the Dorchester. Except they aren't compromises, you know; they are form following function. The phrase I used, 'refined simplicity without perfectionism', is actually simplicity through functionalism, if you prefer a more positive-sounding motto. Maybe gastronomy should be called digestible architecture.

On some preparations, some sources and quantities

A number of recipes in this book suggest the use of certain store-bought preparations, as I was just saying. It's possible to get along without them. When I run out I often do without them, and try to make similar concoctions by hand myself. But they save time, and a few of them have unique flavours impossible to achieve otherwise. Here is a partial list:

Liquid Maggi A savoury sauce of singular flavour useful for steaks and certain other kinds of grill food.
Maggi Ikan Bilis Dried fish granules, the Maggi company's brilliant answer to fish stock.
Cá Cóm (Bangkok fish sauce) Something less than a fish sauce, more than a fish stock. A more provocative flavour than Ikan Bilis, with a powerful natural fishy smell.
Worcestershire sauce Lea & Perrins' extremely versatile mixture of soy and spicy stuff.
Tabasco sauce The McIlhenny Company of Louisiana's fermented chilli sauce.
Dijon mustard Mixes with salad dressings and mayonnaise; indispensable with pork.
Cremona mustard A delicious Italian chutney mixture of mustard and fruits that's great with cold meats like tongue.
Commercial mayonnaise I never use it on its own – well, hardly ever – but a little is often very handy as a suspension agent with Dijon mustard, garlic purée, olive oil, or salad dressing.
Garlic purée This has less strength than hand-chopped garlic, but the latter can't compare in convenience with this stuff from a tube or jar when grilling meat or seafood.
Pancetta The highly bred bacon of Italian gastronomy, usually used finely chopped in tiny amounts.
Matzo meal Sometimes hard to find, but worth looking for

because it's more delicate as a coating or a starch mixer than breadcrumbs.

Some dishes herein were inspired by my Irish mother, others by my Jewish mother-in-law. Unless otherwise specified in the recipes that follow, the quantities given will serve about four people.

1 SOME ROXY SPECIALS

featured at The Three Greyhounds,
The Soho Brasserie and The Unicorn

Barmaids Old and New

POTATO BREAD AND ACCOMPANIMENTS

225g/8oz potatoes cooked in their skins, then peeled and sieved or mashed smoothly – *reserve the potato water*
1 sachet easy-blend dried yeast
360g/12oz plain white bread flour
1½ tablespoons salt
1 tablespoon olive oil

I got the idea for potato bread from Elizabeth David who describes it as a loaf that retains its moisture, is very light and is wonderful for toasting. In fact, its moist open texture makes its toast take butter rather like the American favourite, English muffins. As made by the David recipe, you'd need to be told that potatoes were in the bread. In my version, which I prefer, you notice their flavour. Makes one large loaf or two medium loaves.

Put the sieved potato, yeast, flour, salt and olive oil in a bowl. Slowly add up to 280ml/10fl oz warm potato liquid and blend together to form a dough – you might not need all the liquid. Knead the dough for a few minutes until it is smooth but still soft.

Put the dough in a bowl in a warm place covered with a damp cloth and let rise for about two hours. Then 'knock it back' – distribute the fermenting yeast – by kneading again. Fill a greased 900g/2lb baking tin or two 450g/1lb tins about halfway or a bit higher with the dough. (I use a tin that measures 7.5 x 13 x 25 cm/3 x 5 x 10 inches.) Again let it rise in a warm place, covered with a damp cloth, until the dough is at or nearly at the top of the tin or tins. Bake at 230°C/450°F/Gas 8 oven for about 35 minutes, then bang the loaves out of the tins and allow them to cool on wire racks.

When the loaves are cool, cut into slices about 2cm/¾in thick, toast and serve with one of the following:

spreads of butter and thin Marmite

dribbles of olive oil with strips of cooked red pepper

cold Greek Street Squid Casserole (page 24).

CLAM CHOWDER ROXY

70g/ 2½oz shallots, chopped
15g/½oz butter with 1
    tablespoon olive oil
2 garlic cloves, finely chopped
½ teaspoon crushed dried chilli
½ handful parsley, chopped
170ml/6fl oz white wine
900ml/32fl oz clam liquor and
    fish stock (I use an infusion of
    dried Ikan Bilis – see page 13)
450g/1 lb turnips, diced, using a
    bit of geometrical precision
580g/1 lb 5oz clams (freshly
    steamed or tinned), chopped
    with liquid
4 spring onions, chopped
Chopped dill or coriander,
    optional
4 rashers bacon, fried and
    crumbled, or 3 teaspoons
    pancetta, diced
Pepper, and salt if required

A restaurant critic friend has a memorable dictum: 'Soups aren't sexy'. How true at a Glyndebourne picnic or a little supper à deux! How unnecessarily disallowing at the agreeable prospect of a lobster or oyster bisque, or this dish.

Clams are native to Britain, but largely ignored here. I'm not certain why. Perhaps because oysters and scallops have richer flavour, mussels are more tender. But the wonderful texture and rather subtle taste of clams can be fully enjoyed in a chowder. My own recipe is quite unlike New England or Manhattan clam chowders – partly to reduce the amount of animal fat, partly to achieve a style that could be considered peculiar to Britain, partly to encourage appetite rather than engulf it. Its clear broth and undisintegrating turnips (instead of mushy potatoes) make it look and taste extremely sexy, and in my view the classic American chowders aren't as salutary to an accompanying drink as this one.

This chowder is delicious even if you think you aren't fond of turnips, because the clam flavour decisively alters that slightly metallic taste (which I happen to appreciate in any case). For an alternative in a somewhat different part of the clammy gastronomic spectrum, omit the diced turnips and spring onions and substitute thinly sliced parsnips and coarsely grated carrot, and do use coriander. For full flavour either way, prepare several hours in advance or the day before and reheat.

Sauté the shallots in butter and oil until nearly transparent. Add the garlic and continue to sauté until the garlic is starting to colour, then add the chilli and parsley for a few final seconds. Now add the white wine and boil until the liquid is reduced by a third. Add the clam liquor and fish stock and turnips and simmer until almost tender, then for the last few minutes of simmering add the clams, spring onions and dill or coriander, if using. Season further if necessary; garnish with the bacon or pancetta and serve.

OLD COMPTON OYSTER STEW

5 shallots, finely chopped
110g/3½oz butter
400ml/14fl oz milk
150ml/5fl oz double cream
20-28 frozen oysters (or fresh
    ones shelled, plus their liquor
    strained through muslin)
Salt and ground white pepper
Paprika or crushed dried chilli
2 egg yolks
Chopped parsley, as garnish

Eating oysters raw on the half shell is the great way, and the way most pub customers prefer. In about 1987 I decided to price them singly at The Unicorn because when they were offered in dozens and half-dozens I noticed many couples would share a plate of six. I purveyed a ton of them after that, in twos, threes and fours, at the unheard of price of 55p each. My barmen and I became champion oyster openers. The oysters arriving weekly from the fishmonger were usually a sellout, but if any were left after a few days I would turn them into oyster stew, the second greatest oyster dish. It's a very high cholesterol recipe not suitable for the overweight in their fifties except as a wicked treat, which is exactly what it is.

Certainly, freshness is the prime consideration in oysters eaten raw, for reasons of taste as much as health. But contrary to the general rule with seafood, absolute freshness is so much less a consideration for cooked oysters that a terrific version of oyster stew (I promise) can be made with the frozen Japanese oysters sold in plastic bags for restaurants. These are frozen individually, can be counted out like lumps of white coal, and are out of their shells, which may be their key attribute when one is deficient in the knack of opening oysters. If an oriental supermarket where they are sold is in your vicinity I recommend them for both cheapness (49p per oyster at time of writing) and convenience, and I challenge anyone to detect the oysters came frozen.

Sauté the shallots in the butter. When they become soft but not brown, put them in the top of a double boiler or the top of an improvised bain-marie (one pot within another containing simmering water) because the cream and milk should not boil. Add the milk, cream and oysters to the shallots in the top container. Allow the water to simmer until the creamy liquid is hot and the oysters float, which takes twenty minutes or so. This means the oyster stew is ready. Add salt as necessary, white pepper, and a little paprika or crushed chilli.

To thicken the stew into a bisque, whisk the egg yolks in a bowl, and slowly add a few spoonfuls of the stew liquid to them until the yolks have been cooked and thickened by the heat. Add this to the stew, then serve, garnishing individual bowls with the chopped parsley.

OYSTER SOUP

4 spring onions, chopped
2 small shallots, chopped
2 fresh medium hot chillis,
    chopped
6cm/2½in length of cucumber,
    peeled, seeded and finely
    diced
15g/½oz butter
2 tablespoons Cá Cóm fish sauce,
    or strong fish stock
About 3 tablespoons garlic purée
12-16 fresh oysters with their
    liquor strained through
    muslin, or frozen
Chopped coriander, as garnish

As pleasing as oyster stew only from a quite different territory of tastes, this was inspired by a dish I saw photographed in the Australian foodie magazine *Vogue Entertaining*, a periodical I enjoy, though I think it's more aptly named for its entertainment value than its entertainment ideas – it's full of difficult recipes for bringing about gastronomically complex voodoo flavours. My inspiration was a smoky sour oyster soup made with (according to the picture caption) Pacific oysters, smoked tommy ruff, lemon grass, galangal, chilli, fish sauce, kaffir lime juice, palm sugar and shallots. My pale imitation with mostly common ingredients isn't smoky or sour but delicious nevertheless, and dead easy to do. As I noted with oyster stew (page 18), frozen Pacific oysters can be used without risking flavour deprivation.

Use two medium sauté pans. In one, combine the spring onions, shallots, chillis and cucumber, turn up the heat and swizzle in the butter for about a minute, then add the oyster liquor made up to about 1 litre/1¾ pints with water and the Cá Cóm fish sauce. There you have the stock. In the other pan, quite hot, fry the garlic purée and brown all the oysters in it.

Check the strength of your stock by putting an oyster in a small bowl, adding a few spoonfuls of stock, and tasting. As necessary, reduce the stock a little by boiling at high heat, or add some more water and reheat. Mix stock with oysters and serve in large bowls garnished with chopped coriander.

COARSE POTATO-CORN SOUP

450g/1lb floury potatoes, peeled
  and diced
2 shallots, chopped
55g/2oz butter
280ml/10fl oz dry white wine
290g/10oz cooked sweetcorn
  kernels
Salt and ground white pepper
3 tablespoons single cream
Chopped coriander, as garnish

I admit this soup isn't sexy, but neither is a loving grandma. This is a very simple tasty dish. The only thing is, don't make it on the day you want to serve it. It becomes twice as good twenty-four hours after it is made, I don't know exactly why. It must have something to do with the potato and corn starches needing that long to intermingle and turn themselves into a joint flavour effort. After a day the soup is delicious hot, and if served cold it becomes a Vichyssoise with real personality.

In a sauté pan, swizzle the potatoes and shallots in the butter and allow to cook over a low heat until the onions are soft and the potatoes are just beginning to colour. Add the wine. Boil off the alcohol, then add about 1 litre/1¾ pints water and most of the corn – reserve about 3 tablespoonfuls. Simmer for about an hour, then mash the visible potato lumps in the pan with a masher, not worrying about achieving puréed perfection (this is a *coarse* soup). Season, and set aside until the following day.

When ready to serve, warm up the soup just to medium-hot (unless it's to be served cold), correcting the seasoning if necessary. Add whirls of cream and ladle it into bowls, garnishing with the reserved corn and the chopped coriander.

SOUR ONION TARTE TATIN

4 large red onions, finely sliced
3 tablespoons plain vegetable oil
   without noticeable taste,
   such as groundnut oil
1 tablespoon red wine vinegar,
   plus a few drops of balsamic
   vinegar
Salt and coarsely ground black
   pepper
1 teaspoon Maggi liquid
   seasoning
1 packet frozen puff pastry
Chopped coriander, as garnish
Crushed dried chilli, optional

The Tatin sisters gave their name to tarts cooked upside-down when they made them famous in their French hotel about a hundred years ago. Rather than an apple tart like theirs, this is a savoury one with the onion also benefiting from the caramelising that happens when it is cooked next to the metal. A sour onion tart makes a really simple but impressive and delicious starter.

A word about one of the ingredients, Maggi liquid seasoning. It's made of hydrolysed vegetable protein, salt and soy sauce, but that no more describes its unique taste than Coca-Cola's ingredients do. Like Coke, Maggi is also internationally available, and I hear from friends it's extremely big in the Far East, Mexico, Poland, even France (a few drops of Maggi on a steak provides a great French bistro taste). Maggi adds a decisive *je ne sais quoi* to the flavour of this tart, but if you can't get hold of it don't bother trying any substitutes because there really aren't any. On the frozen puff pastry, chefs all use it; making your own pâte feuilletée is difficult and I won't attempt to describe the procedure.

Stew, rather than fry, the sliced onions in the oil. When soft, add the vinegar, salt, pepper, and the Maggi, which will impart an instant Left Bank identity to the proceedings. Place the onions into the bottom of a round baking tin or casserole – perhaps one of those shallow round enamelled steel pans with sloping sides – about 25cm/10in diameter. (When multiplying this recipe to make canapés for many, use a big square baking tin and afterwards cut the tart into squares.) Roll out enough pastry to about 0.3cm/⅛in thick and cut it to fit snugly over the onion mixture.

Bake for 30 minutes at 175°C/350°F/Gas 4. Turn the baking tin or pan upside down and pound it to make the tart drop out. Serve warm or cold with a garnish of chopped coriander, and if wished, a sprinkle of crushed chilli.

THE ENGLISH CHANNEL SALAD

28 baked dough ball croûtons, about 2.5cm/1in wide (see text)

3 Little Gem or other sensitive-looking and delicious lettuces, sliced radially lengthwise into wedges no more than 2.5cm/1in wide

1 large bulb fennel, sliced very thinly on a mandolin or in a food processor

150-200g/5-7oz Gruyère cheese, coarsely grated by hand

2 hardboiled eggs, coarsely chopped

110g/4oz Westphalian, Black Forest, Palma, York, honey roast or other good ham, cold, either in paper-thin slices if smoked, or sliced into julienne strips 5cm/2in wide

Crushed dried chilli

For the dressing:

3 tablespoons white wine vinegar

110ml/3½floz sunflower or other mild oil

2 teaspoons chopped tarragon

2 teaspoons dried fennel seeds (important to boost the fennel flavour)

4 teaspoons Dijon mustard

Salt and ground black pepper

One night in 1995 my husband and I were in a London hotel restaurant eating authentically made Caesar salads. As many know, this rightly world-famous dish was invented by a restaurateur in Tijuana, Mexico. Our appreciation started us thinking about the possible invention of our own 'signature salad'.

My husband said that when he was an art student he practically lived on the chef's salads that were featured at several Greenwich Village coffee shops: strips of ham and cheese over lettuce in a mustardy vinaigrette. The cheese was processed American and I reckon the mustard was the overteased US confection, so here's the more sophisticated version we developed. Very delicious and it's become extremely popular. If ours has a claim to the salad pantheon, it's because it contrives an excuse for a magisterial assemblage of harmonious flavours: fennel (augmented by tarragon), Gruyère, mustard and cold roast ham. A French cheese would be more geographically appropriate, but I think Gruyère is perfect with fennel.

The Channel (the salad is named to commemorate the Chunnel, and multimedia) is poetically symbolised by our round croûtons, which are shaped like channel buoys. We first tried it at The Three Greyhounds with little hot baked dough balls made from pizza dough provided by the kitchen at Kettner's round the corner, to which we added some fennel seeds – ten minutes in the oven and they were baked to order perfectly. Now we make our own dough balls using durum wheat and fennel seeds – they are the most memorable ingredient. As substitutes, the recipe could use commercial ball-shaped soup croûtons, commercial disc-shaped toast croûtons, or Taralli al Seme di Finocchio, an alternative from Italian grocers (that is, Italian pretzels flavoured with fennel – they bear out the Channel theme by being sort of life-preserver shaped). You might also make your own bagel dough, roll bits of it into balls the size of large marbles and boil them. The task is achieving a starchy component that looks quite different from Caesar croûtons, as any of the above will do. Hail Caesar, anyway.

A technology note: this dish requires an ultra-hot fire applied to the cheese once it is on the plate. An overhead gas grill or salamander is really too general in its effect because it will heat up the whole salad – though in a pinch, use that. I've suggested a butane blowlamp (sometimes used by chefs when making crèmes brûlées). But the most practical tool is a gas-fired Bunsen burner, because you won't have to buy replacement butane canisters or need to worry about possible explosive leaks. Have a plumber install an extra gas cock in your kitchen, to which you fit a flexible tube and a Bunsen burner (various designs are available from laboratory suppliers). As a Bunsen burner provides an extremely hot, focused jet of flame, you'll find it a handy way to deal with lots of pesky cooking requirements: caramelising sugar, charring pinfeathers and scorching pepper skins, as well as melting cheese on English Channel salads.

Put the dressing ingredients in a jar and shake together at least half an hour before the salad is to be served to release flavour from the fennel seeds. If the croûtons are excessively crisp and pretzel-like, soften them a little in the dressing.

Toss the lettuce, fennel, croûtons and half the grated cheese with the dressing (don't use a stingier proportion of cheese than indicated) and distribute on to serving plates. Sprinkle the egg decorously on top of each. Arrange the ham strips on top of that, then the reserved half of the grated cheese on top of that with the crushed chilli uppermost.

Just before the salads are served, give the covering cheese a 30-second blast with a butane blowlamp – or a horizontally-held Bunsen burner – until it gets soft and begins to look runny and the chilli bits blacken; alternatively, the chilli can be added after melting. Try not to heat up anything but the covering cheese, though the ham might become slightly warmed, and take care not to crack the plates. After another 30 seconds all butane smell will have disappeared (you needn't worry about cooking gas with the Bunsen burner) and the dishes can be promptly served.

GREEK STREET SQUID CASSEROLE

Olive oil
2 large onions, or 6-8 shallots,
    finely chopped
5 garlic cloves, finely chopped
1.3kg/3lb squid, cleaned and
    sliced
4 red peppers, seeded
About half a bottle red wine
2-4 plum tomatoes, skinned, or
    200ml/7fl oz passata, or
    75ml/3fl oz sundried tomato
    tapenade
Salt and ground black pepper
Thinly chopped leeks (optional)
Chopped parsley or coriander
1 teaspoon crushed dried chilli

I thought I invented this myself during the summer of 1991. Then in 1994, I saw a newspaper cooking column which mentioned a similar-sounding dish that appears in Anton Mosimann's *Fish Cuisine*. I haven't checked because I've never seen that book, and my version seems quite appreciated. Serve this with polenta, taglierini or saffron rice. This dish is noticeably more delicious the second day, and it is also good unheated with Potato Bread (page 16). This serves six.

For the selection and cleaning of squid, see p. 25. In some olive oil in a deep saucepan, sauté the onions and the garlic until golden, add the sliced squid and sauté until it begins to brown, then add strips of peppers and turn up the heat to evaporate most of the liquid. Cover with red wine and reduce heat to a simmer. Add tomatoes, seasoning, and leeks if you are using them. Half cover the pan and simmer for 45-60 minutes. Add the parsley or coriander and chilli as garnishes just before serving.

GRILLED SQUID AND INK RISOTTO

I first made this as Christmas dinner on a romantic holiday in Miami in a motel room with saucepans over an electric ring, so it can be done anywhere. Since then, I've found that squid grills extremely well on my caterer's charcoal grill (see page 101 for further details), but it's easy to do – probably easier – on a domestic gas grill with the flames overhead. Either way the grilling is super-quick so, after you clean the squid, make the risotto before you cook the squid.

8-10 small squid with bodies 10-12.5cm/4-5in long (these are the tenderest)
200ml/7fl oz sesame oil
½ teaspoon crushed dried chilli

For the risotto:
1 litre/1¾ pints fish stock, which can be made with dissolved Ikan Bilis granules
45g/1½oz butter
1 tablespoon garlic purée, or 3 garlic cloves, finely chopped
250g/9oz carnaroli or arborio rice
Squid ink saved from cleaning them, or 2 expensive little sachets of squid, octopus or cuttlefish ink
Salt and ground black pepper
Handful coriander or parsley, chopped
2 tablespoons sesame seeds

Clean the squid by first rinsing them in running water, then pulling each head with the tentacles away from the bag-shaped body. You can (but needn't) peel the thin outer membrane off the body. Within the head section, pull away and discard the cartilage that looks like clear plastic, then cut off the tentacles below the eyes, keeping the tentacles connected to each other and discarding the section with the eyes. Feel within the tentacles and remove the hard mouth. Each squid has now been transformed into a clean body sack and a clean set of tentacles – can any of us say better! Give them a final rinse and a bit of a dry on a clean tea towel, then marinate them in the sesame oil with crushed chilli.

To make the risotto, unfreeze some of your prepared fish stock or make one with Ikan Bilis granules in water with some of the coriander. In a sauté pan over moderate heat, melt the butter with the garlic and swizzle round the risotto rice until the grains are all hot and coated. Slowly begin adding the fish stock while stirring. After about 15 minutes check the texture by tasting. When the grains are nearly al dente add the squid ink and let them absorb it. Turn off the heat, add the seasoning and most of the chopped coriander and give a quick stir, then cover the pan.

Grill the squid by placing the highly oiled pieces on (or under) a very hot grill, using a brick to flatten them if you have the heat coming from underneath. They need only about 90 seconds on each side; a bit longer with an overhead grill. After removing, quickly slice the bodies into rings and the tentacle sections once or twice the long way.

In a separate dry sauté pan, slightly brown the sesame seeds as a garnish. Serve the risotto with sesame seeds on top with the grilled squid alongside, sprinkled with the last of the chopped coriander. Hoi sin sauce from an oriental supermarket is a possible accompaniment, but if the fish stock is flavoursome it's unnecessary.

FOUR-MEAT LOAF

2 tablespoons vegetable oil
500g/18oz veal off the bone,
 coarsely chopped
4 tablespoons sunflower seeds
1kg/2½lb minced lean beef
500g/18oz minced pork
3 medium onions *and* 5 large
 garlic cloves, finely chopped
 together
250ml/9fl oz gherkins sliced or
 pimiento-stuffed green olives
6-7 tablespoons tomato purée, or
 moist sundried tomatoes
110g/4oz matzo meal crumbs or
 wheat germ, moistened in
 wine or beer
1 handful parsley, chopped
½ handful fresh basil, chopped,
 or 1 tablespoon dried basil
3 or 4 eggs
Salt and ground black pepper
400g/14oz sweet cured streaky
 bacon, rinded
Wine or beer for basting

When I served roast meat at The Unicorn, anything left over was chopped up semi-coarsely and added to the next day's meat loaf. The chunks of dark brown roast meat looked wonderful in the meat loaf's sliced cross-section, and a roast I used to cook a lot of in those days, pork chops in ketchup, Worcestershire sauce and lemon juice, lent it something special.

Which is a way of saying that in my opinion, meat loaf should be a cross between a country pâté and a leftover surprise. The fear and loathing of leftovers in cooking is just contemporary supermarket mentality, unsupported by classic gastronomy, genuine principles of health or the conservation of resources.

But oh, all right. Here's how to make a brilliant meat loaf without relying on leftovers, though I insist that the judicious addition of some (always using good judgement, mind) would be perfectly fine. This quantity will serve ten to twelve people. As it's best served cold or cool, that shouldn't present any difficulties – you won't find leftover meat loaf hanging around for long.

In a heavy pan, heat the vegetable oil to a medium-high temperature and sauté the veal chunks until well browned. Add the sunflower seeds, stir around and turn off the heat.

In a mixing bowl, combine the veal, seeds and all other ingredients except the bacon and wine or beer, mixing and squeezing with your hands. Form into a long curve-topped loaf down the centre of a large baking tin, allowing a gutter either side for fat to run off. Cover the top of the loaf with a blanket of strips of bacon, tucking the loose ends under.

Roast at 175°C/350°F/Gas 4 for about 1¾ hours, basting occasionally with wine or beer. Serve cool or cold without the fat that's seeped out and accumulated along the sides, along with prepared ketchup, horseradish sauce, Cumberland sauce or chopped gherkins.

SWEETBREAD CASSEROLE

1.3kg/3lb lamb sweetbreads
Court bouillon made from water
    with chopped onion, celery,
    carrot and bay leaf
45g/1½oz butter
1 onion, sliced
1 carrot, thinly sliced
1 celery stick, thinly sliced
1 bay leaf
6 sprigs fresh thyme, or 1
    teaspoon dried thyme
½ handful parsley, chopped
1 teaspoon flour
Salt and ground black pepper
150ml/5fl oz white wine
165g/6oz petits pois
2 tablespoons Madeira

Here's a wonderfully delicious casserole that is simple to make, adapted from a sadly out-of-print book called *Offal* by two San Francisco food writers[5]. It makes a perfect pub lunch with French bread.

Before BSE, most people only encountered sweetbreads in the form of sliced, breaded deep-fried veal ones. But lamb sweetbreads are what should be used for this dish. They are much cheaper than veal, their taste seems to work better in this context, they are readily obtainable frozen (without much flavour penalty so it's a good way to buy them) and the simple prep of poaching gets rid of some of the cholesterol by removing all the surrounding fat. This casserole will serve six.

Soak and wash the sweetbreads thoroughly in running water, removing any bloody bits, discolorations and superfluous tubes, and cutting large pieces in half. Poach in the court bouillon for five minutes. Reserve about 225ml/8fl oz of the liquid (and retain and freeze the rest of it for subsequent makings of the recipe, or for other rich stock uses).

Melt the butter in a flameproof casserole and sauté the onion, carrot and celery for about 10 minutes until they are lightly browned, finally stirring in the herbs and flour. Salt and pepper the sweetbreads and lay them on top of the vegetables. Add the wine and reserved liquid, using no more than needed to barely cover the sweetbreads, and bring the casserole to a boil. Cover the casserole and put it in a preheated 175°C/350°F/Gas 4 oven for an hour, checking after a few minutes to make sure the casserole is just simmering. Ten minutes before the end of the cooking time, add the peas and Madeira and adjust the seasoning. Serve with buttered French bread.

---

5 Jana Allen & Margaret Gin, *Offal*, London 1976.

SPICED OX TONGUE WITH BROAD BEANS

1 spiced ox tongue, weighing
    1.3-2kg/3-4½lb

For the court bouillon:
1 onion, stuck with 3 cloves
3 garlic cloves, mashed
1 bay leaf
½ lemon
Several sprigs parsley

Spiced ox tongues can occasionally be found at my supermarket, and almost always to be found at Selfridges meat department in London. The spicing is a mild curing in pickling or corning brine, usually with bay, juniper, mace and pepper, that adds something to the meat well worth having added. I prefer it to smoked ox tongue. Served hot, it goes well with a bit of Dijon mustard and broad beans in white sauce (see recipe below). And, of course, it is also delicious served cold.

If you cater for two people, a lovely idea is to have the tongue hot at one meal and cold for a later meal. When it's hot, carve the tongue starting from the root end. After the meal, curl up the rest of the meat starting with the tongue tip, squeeze it into a round bowl or tin with vertical sides and refrigerate – the tongue gelatine will set it. When ready to serve it as cold cuts, unmould it from the bowl and carve slices with a spiral pattern by cutting across the circular top. Serve it the second time with a garnish of either sauce gribiche (similar to mayonnaise with mashed hard-boiled eggs, herbs, and capers), or, better yet, with a few spoon-fuls of Cremona mustard, a bittersweet mustard-flavoured fruit chutney obtainable from Italian grocers, and with hot mashed potatoes.

Rinse the tongue and place it in a pan covered with water to cover. Bring to the boil, then allow to simmer for 5 minutes and skim off scum from surface. Add the court bouillon ingredients and simmer until tender, which will take about 110 minutes per kilo/50 minutes per pound. (If, however, you are cooking a fresh unspiced tongue, use just onion, celery, carrot and a bay leaf for the court bouillon.)

Remove the tongue from the liquid and, after a few minutes to let it cool slightly, peel off all the outer skin, which is very easy using a thin pointed knife – it gets quite loose. Trim up the root end in the kitchen, tasting, not wasting, the bits. A classic way to serve is propped up on hidden wedges of toast, tip of tongue waving gaily at guests (see cover photograph).

Hot or cold, tongue should be carved thinly. Serve slices with one or two spoonfuls of the broth on each plate. Save the rest of the liquid for reheating the tongue, or curl up the tongue in a close-fitting bowl with vertical sides and refrigerate. The spiced tongue broth will be too salty to retain for meat stock, but is useful in small quantities in the following recipe for broad beans. Unspiced tongue broth *is* fine as a basis for stock and worth saving.

BROAD BEANS IN WHITE SAUCE

2.25kg/5lb small and tender unshelled broad beans, or 600g/22oz frozen broad beans

For the white sauce:
30g/1oz butter
2 tablespoons flour
170ml/6fl oz milk and no more than about 55ml/2fl oz ox tongue broth combined
2 teaspoons celery seeds
½ handful parsley, chopped
Salt and ground white pepper

Shell the beans. Bring a pan of salted water to a rolling boil and cook the beans until tender: with fresh beans it depends on their size – it could take 10 minutes, 20, or even longer; frozen beans will take about 5 minutes, but follow the packet's advice.

For the white sauce, melt the butter in a pan, add the flour and stir over low heat for a few moments. Slowly stir in the milk with a little of the milk and tongue mixture – no more than a quarter should be tongue broth or the sauce will be too salty – letting the butter and flour thicken the liquid. Add the celery seeds and chopped parsley and adjust the seasoning as necessary. Serve with a pool of sauce flooding halfway over the beans and the hot tongue.

SMOKED CHICKEN AND AVOCADO IN OLIVE OIL

1 prepared smoked chicken
4 or 5 medium avocados, not
  overmushy
150ml/5fl oz best extra virgin
  olive oil
Salt and ground black pepper
Flat-leaf parsley, chopped, as
  garnish

As I recall, smoked chickens started appearing in the markets about fifteen years ago – first from France, and now from domestic sources. I think their smoky flavour isn't enormously delicate, but on the other hand they benefit very well from some emollient additions.

A smoked chicken will serve four nicely in this buffet-style party piece that is also good as a picnic main course. It's an assembled rather than a cooked dish, so it makes a perfect assignment for a day when you (or a teenage helper) would feel enriched by accomplishing something that's neat and organised.

The day before serving, or at least several hours ahead, cut all the meat off the chicken in slices as thin and wide as you can make them. Stone and peel the avocados and slice them thinly.

Using a big platter and starting from the edge, make a spiral of alternating chicken and avocado slices, periodically dribbling olive oil over both. Salt and pepper lightly and garnish with parsley. Cover with cling film or foil and allow to rest for a few hours or refrigerate overnight so the oil soaks in.

STEAK TARTARE AND GARLIC CIABATTA

Garlic bread first appeared on my pub's blackboard by accident when the food for a planned accompaniment wasn't delivered. Prior to that, I had thought that garlic bread alone was too simple to sell. Wrong. When it appears, all Old Compton Street is garlicked to the nines until I tire of making it and remove it from the board.

2 egg yolks
150ml/5fl oz extra virgin olive oil
900g/2lb chopped fillet of beef
    or other lean steak (texture is
    important: should be hand-
    chopped or very lightly
    processor-chopped, not
    ground in a commercial or
    home meat grinder)
2 onions, chopped
1½ handfuls parsley, chopped
1½ teaspoons salt
2 tablespoons capers, chopped if
    they are large
6 anchovy fillets in oil, chopped
3 dashes Tabasco sauce, or ½
    teaspoon crushed dried chilli
1 teaspoon chopped fresh dill,
    but omit dill altogether if it
    isn't fresh

For the garlic ciabatta:
8 thick slices ciabatta bread
110g/4oz butter
110g/4oz garlic purée
Black peppercorns, roughly
    crushed or very coarsely
    ground
½ handful parsley, chopped

My version is not the half-sliced standard French stick toasted in foil in the oven, because if the bread is really great, there's no need for it even to be toasted. Italian ciabatta is the answer: it's a wonderful heavy but fluffy white bread made with olive oil. All it needs are generous spreads of butter and prepared garlic purée, then into the microwave for 30 seconds. Chefs always apologise when they mention a perfect use for a microwave so I wish to tender my apology here. Nevertheless, when a platter of my sliced rounds of garlic ciabatta sprinkled with parsley comes out of the kitchen and the wonderful smell permeates the bar, the beer drinkers just impulsively order it. So would anybody.

Steak tartare has more particular admirers. If you love the taste of good beef (as many don't, not really), steak tartare is the mother of beef dishes. It is simply about the unparalleled flavour of beef, which you eat raw because you love it. Make it only from proper lean steak – lean steak is also most likely to circumvent Bovine Spongiform Encephalopathy hazards, if you worry about that as I do – and don't louse it up with anything that will disguise the fresh pure beef flavour. So, no Worcestershire sauce, no mustard, no Cognac or other alcoholic additions for this one. Keep the textures somewhat coarse and make the mixture as airy as possible. Garlic ciabatta seems the perfect accompaniment.

For the steak tartare, start with the yolks and olive oil in a large bowl, whipping them up a bit as if they were on the way to becoming mayonnaise, then fork in the chopped beef and other ingredients. Without going on too long, mash them all lightly together, almost folding them together. The tartare needs a lot of air folded in to keep it from becoming a clay-like lump – the slightly coarse textures should help that.

For the garlic ciabatta, spread the thick slices of bread with butter and garlic purée and sprinkle with pepper. Microwave on high power for 30-45 seconds, then sprinkle copiously with chopped parsley. Several ice cream scoops of steak tartare with two slices of garlic ciabatta per person will get the neighbourhood singing your praises.

Dishes using drink

Isn't using drink in food expensive? Not necessarily. At home, one should save wine dregs and leftovers in beer bottles gone flat. In pubs, normal beer handling produces some ullage – that is, draining away of drink. The drink can't be put back, but it can be used productively.

Good management keeps ullage to a minimum, but there is a lot of supply to contend with. The Three Greyhounds is a small bar that holds only about 45 customers when comfortably full. For that number, we usually keep on tap ten 18-gallon 'kilns', i.e., barrels, of lager (four of Carlsberg, five or six other), some Adnams real ale in 18-gallon kilns, and about ten other real ales racked in 9-gallon 'firkins'. Guinness and cider come in 11-gallon cylinders, and generally four Guinness and three cider are standing by.

On Friday mornings, after Eamonn the Drayman comes with his delivery at six, I clean the pipes. I turn off the keg taps and I pull off the liquid in the tubing with the hand pumps – about two pints per beer line. Those quantities of Guinness, cider and lager, which are the pasteurised pressurised beverages, can't be sold or put back. I save them up in the fridge. Here are some recipes that work really well with the first two. For the way I use up my lager ullage, see the batter of my fish and chips recipe (page 64). As for the unpasteurised real ale ullage, I save it for lunch and the staff and I drink it.

Opposite:
Four-Meat Loaf, page 26

WHAT TO DO WITH WINE ENDS

The two best dishes using wine are Coq au Vin, which I often make using a complicated recipe of Julia Child's, and Entrecôte Bordelaise with beef marrow, which doesn't have much wine in it really.

Wine is often used as part of a marinade to flavour and soften the main ingredient of a dish. After soaking venison, for example, in a wine marinade, the seasoned liquid is usually included in the cooking.

Another good way to use the ends of a few bottles of red wine is to make a classic stew such as Boeuf à la Bourguignonne, which at its best should have some prior marinating of the meat and separate cooking of ingredients. I won't guide you on how to do any of these in this book since recipes are easy to find elsewhere.

Meat cooked in wine seasoned with herbs is known as a daube in traditional French cooking. The daube liquid often becomes so jellified it can be carved and served cold as well as hot. Although delicious, daubes are quite simple. In fact, I think of mine as a Dumb Daube: it appears in Chapter 2 on page 60, because a beef stew definitely has to be listed as one of the English pub Top Ten.

Left:
Pie and Pea Floater, page 36;
South Pacific Non-Calorific or
Seafood Frittata, page 42

GUINNESS STEW

900g/2lb stewing steak, all fat trimmed off and cubed
110g/4oz flour mixed with salt and ground black pepper
110ml/3½fl oz olive oil
1 large onion, finely chopped
560ml/20fl oz (that's an English pint, or a bit more) Guinness
450g/1lb mushrooms, cut into large chunks
450g/1lb carrots, scraped and cut into large chunks
1 orange spiked with 2 cloves
1 bay leaf
1½ teaspoons dry mustard
1 tablespoon brown sugar
Chopped parsley, as garnish

Any brew can be substituted in this simple recipe, but Guinness turns into a particularly smooth and delicious stew liquid. It becomes richer and darker than when it started. The small amount of brown sugar counteracts any bitterness the Guinness and cloves might impart. Doing this at home, I'd advise not waiting for the cleanup after a wasteful party – just buy some Guinness. You might wisely make it a day ahead because the usual better-the-next-day homily applies. It goes excellently with pearl barley, boiled potatoes or brown rice, and buttery spinach.

Shake the cubed beef in a plastic bag containing the seasoned flour. Heat the olive oil in a heavy-bottomed pan and swizzle in the onion, then add the floured meat. Brown the meat without letting the flour burn. When just brown on all sides, pour over the Guinness and add the mushrooms, carrots, cloved orange and bay leaf. Simmer for two hours.

At the end of the cooking time, discard the orange. Assess the amount of liquid remaining and either leave it alone, pour a bit off, or top up with some water. Stir in the mustard and sugar, bring back briefly to the boil and correct the seasoning. Garnish with chopped parsley when serving.

CIDER WITH PORK

110g/4oz butter
900g/2lb pork, trimmed of fat
    and cubed
4 shallots, peeled but left whole
4 celery sticks, diced
2 Bramley or other large cooking
    apples, cored, peeled and
    chopped
1 tablespoon juniper berries
Salt and ground black pepper
About 1 litre/1¾ pints cider
110ml/3½fl oz single cream
    (optional)

For the noodles:
340g/12oz fresh or dried
    tagliatelle
45g/1½oz butter
Salt and ground black pepper
1 tablespoon poppy seeds

Young people (also some drunks) love cider. It was quite cheap until extra excise tax was added in 1995. British ciders can be very strong. The cloudy cask-conditioned cider I sell has about 5 percent alcohol, stronger than most beers, and some ciders that are sold in cans off-license are 8½ percent alcohol. 'White Lightning', one is called. We refer to it as 'Brain Damage'. I favour the cooking possibilities of cider, where the alcohol, of course, evaporates.

In a heavy-based pan with a lid, melt the butter over moderate heat and roll the cubes of pork and shallots around in it until the pork changes colour on all sides. Add the celery, apples, juniper berries and some seasoning and sauté for a few moments. Pour in enough cider to cover the ingredients. Put the lid on the pan and simmer for two hours.

When ready to serve, boil another pan of water and cook the tagliatelle until just al dente. Drain and toss them in butter and poppy seeds. If using the optional cream in the stew, reduce the stewing liquid if necessary and stir the cream in just before serving. Correct the seasoning. Serve the pork stew alongside the noodles.

PIE AND PEA FLOATER

450g/1lb stewing steak, trimmed of all fat and chopped
1 onion, chopped
4 carrots, chopped
560ml/20fl oz beer
Salt and ground black pepper
1 packet frozen puff pastry
1 beef stock cube
30g/1oz butter for beurre manié
2 tablespoons flour for beurre manié
225g/8oz frozen petits pois or tinned marrow peas

This late night urban Australian treat for drunks and revellers probably stems from Adelaide, but is also the speciality of Harry's Café de Wheels (it's a caravan) in Woolloomooloo, Sydney. The name refers to Australian meat pies, floating in gravy and peas. The commercially prepared meat pies of Australia have no equal abroad. Big Ben, Four & Twenty, Sargeants, Dransfields – all wonderful. This is my refined attempt for the pub and domestic table.

You need a 12-cup cupcake tin. Stew the meat, onion and carrots in the beer for an hour. Remove the meat, onion and some of the carrots and put them into a bowl. Pull the meat into small pieces with two forks, add a bit of stock to moisten but keep it pretty dry, then season. This is the contents of the meat pies. Shortening is provided by the pastry, and extra taste by the gravy – herbal additions such as thyme are optional, but aren't authentic or really necessary.

Roll out the pastry to about 0.3cm/⅛in thick and use it to line all the cupcake cups. Add the dryish mixture of meat, onion and carrot, cover with puff pastry lids of the same thickness and pinch closed round the edges. Bake for 30 minutes in a 175°C/350°F/Gas 4 oven.

Now turn to the gravy. Either remove the remaining carrots, mash them and put them back in the liquid, or if you have a hand blender, mash them in the pot. Add the beef stock cube dissolved in about 280ml/10fl oz hot water. Thicken the gravy with five or six marble-sized balls of beurre manié made from kneaded flour and butter, dropped one at a time into the reheated gravy as you stir. When ready to serve, add the frozen peas (if using them) to the gravy and simmer for three minutes, or add the tinned peas and just warm them through. Serve the peas and gravy in bowls with two pies floating in each, keeping a third pie in reserve for seconds.

CHEESE AND ONION PIE

4 onions, thinly sliced
450g/1lb mild Cheddar cheese, thinly sliced (processed Crackerjack is good)
Salt and pepper
Dabs of butter or mayonnaise
1 egg, beaten

For the rich shortcrust pastry:
110g/4oz chilled butter, diced
200g/7oz plain flour
1 teaspoon salt
2 tablespoons iced water

This is an old family favourite: my mother's picnic special. Perhaps it isn't particularly Australian since I knew of no one else who made it – they all wanted Mrs Hoffmann's pie. It sure isn't a contender for the slimline award, but I like to imagine that the onions help to ameliorate the cholesterol. It's best eaten warm, served with a green salad and beer.

Make a very buttery shortcrust pastry in the food processor: put the butter, flour and salt in the bowl and process until coarse crumbs form. Drizzle in the water through the feed tube and continue processing just until the crumbs come together. Don't overprocess or the pastry will be tough. Wrap and chill for one hour.

Roll out the pastry to about 0.3cm/⅛in. Butter a round meat pie tin or casserole and line it with pastry, saving part of the pastry for a lid.

Fill with layers of the raw onions and cheese alternatively, sprinkling with lots of salt and ground black pepper, and dabs of butter or mayonnaise. Cover with the pastry lid and brush with egg for a handsome glaze. Bake in a 150°C/300°F/Gas 2 oven for 45 minutes.

MELBOURNE MOWBRAY PIE

900g/2lb pie veal, all fat trimmed
    off and neatly cubed
    (because we're going to see
    the neat pieces clearly in the
    aspic)
110-165g/4-6oz good gammon or
    ham, neatly cubed
3 hardboiled eggs
1 handful parsley, chopped
1½ teaspoons ground nutmeg
Salt and ground black pepper

For the shortcrust pastry:
165g/6oz butter, at room
    temperature
450g/1lb plain flour
½ teaspoon salt
3 egg yolks
Juice of 1 lemon
Ground black pepper

For the aspic:
Veal bones
6 sticks celery with leaves
1 carrot, cut lengthwise
1 large onion, quartered
10 black peppercorns
Bouquet garni of parsley,
    tarragon, thyme and 2 bay
    leaves
1 or 2 sachets powdered gelatine
    (if necessary)

Melton Mowbray, a small town up the A1, was the home of a famous version of that English classic, the cold pork-in-aspic pie. Jane Grigson's book on English food says the pieworks closed in 1972. Nevertheless, if you mooch around to the Fortnum & Mason food hall and buy a slice of one of theirs that still goes by the generic name, you can probably detect some, or all, of the famous MM's ingredients: boned pork, sage, nutmeg, cinnamon, allspice, pink bacon for colour, gelatine, and the secret ingredient, some anchovy essence.

Meanwhile in a far-off galaxy, colonial cooks who never visited Melton Mowbray created an alternative version which – despite lacking intense flavours like pork and anchovy essence – was certainly not poorer. When I ate some of my tryout sample it was like Proust's Madeleine: the long-ago returned, tasteable, though my mother made the pie only about once in five years. She made it for father when they were courting in 1937.

Her recipe was adapted from *The Kookaburra Cookery Book*[6], and here it is. The pastry is very short (there's lots of butter). Some of the pie's unique flavour is from the lemon juice and egg yolks in the pastry. The veal aspic is also magical, especially if your butcher will give you *a lot* of bones. The pie is eaten cold. Cumberland sauce is the classic accompaniment, but isn't mandatory. I've called this Melbourne Mowbray Pie, though it's a place not found on any map.

You should use a 20cm/8in spring clip cake tin for this, and a ceramic pie chimney is handy. (I have a ceramic blackbird.) An overview of the whole process is as follows: (1) make the pastry and chill it for several hours or overnight; (2) line the tin with the pastry, put in the dry meat and eggs, cover with a pastry lid and bake; (3) pour in the liquid veal aspic, filling the voids in the pie; (4) allow the aspic to set.

For the pastry, rub the butter into the flour with the salt, then

---

6 This book, a cultural monument one day perhaps to the academically plumbed, was published in 1928. The recipes are contributions from the women of South Australia to an anonymous editor at the Lady Victoria Buxton Girls' Club.

make a well in the mixture and gradually pour in a little chilled water. As the pastry becomes kneadable, add the egg yolks, lemon juice and pepper. Add enough extra water to have a good pliable pastry. Leave the ball of dough in the refrigerator for 2-36 hours.

For the veal aspic, put the veal bones in a large saucepan or stockpot, cover with water and boil for five minutes, then turn off the heat and remove any scum. Return to a simmer, adding the vegetables and bouquet garni, then simmer for at least four hours, allowing the liquid to reduce by about a third. Strain out the bones and vegetables and pour off the fat. If the bones contained a lot of gelatine you may not actually need to add any extra, but playing safe, use 45g/1½oz powdered gelatine to jellify 560ml/20fl oz stock. Soak the gelatine in about a cupful of the stock, then stir it into the liquid following the packet instructions.

When ready to bake, roll out the pastry with a rolling pin and line the tin with two thirds of it – the quantity of butter will make this easy to do with your fingers. Pack the filling of raw meat and hardboiled eggs with parsley and nutmeg and seasoning firmly in the pastry shell, around the ceramic pie chimney if using one. Cover with the remaining pastry, pinching securely round the sides and cutting a little hole over the chimney. Make decorations with some flat remnants of pastry, sticking them on with a little water: birds, a family, faces, geometrical or astronomical shapes. Include in the design a 2cm/¾in hole (in addition to the pie chimney hole) for inserting a funnel after the pie is baked.

Bake in a 175°C/350°F/Gas 4 oven for three hours. Remove and allow to cool for about an hour, then insert a funnel and fill the pie with the warm liquid veal aspic, tilting the pie a bit to get it into all the voids. Put in the refrigerator until the aspic has set, then unclip and remove the cake tin. Serve by slicing out wedges with a sharp knife.

COLD POACHED LOIN OF PORK AND ONION MARMALADE

1 boned loin of pork without crackling, rolled and tied
Half handfuls each of 2 or 3 available fresh mild herbs, such as parsley, tarragon and thyme, but not strong tasting ones like mint, fennel or caraway
1 teaspoon celery seeds
1 bay leaf
10 whole peppercorns
2 cloves garlic, peeled and squashed
120ml/4fl oz malt vinegar
110g/4oz brown sugar

This is a very simple method of cooking pork that maximises flavour and minimises fat. The recipe for Onion Marmalade is on page 127.

Weigh the pork loin before you start cooking. Put the meat in a stewing pot much larger than the joint, cover with water and bring to the boil. After two or three minutes, turn off the heat and remove any scum and fat. Add all the rest of the ingredients and bring the heat back to a simmer. Cook for 1 hour per kilo/25 minutes per pound.

Cool, then refrigerate the pork loin in its stewing liquid. Slice thinly to serve with onion marmalade, and possibly a spiced orange chutney. A green salad and hot butter beans in parsley are other reasonable accompaniments.

CARPETBAG STEAK (WITH OYSTERS)

A long squeeze of garlic purée, or 4 garlic cloves, finely chopped
45g/1½oz butter
8-10 oysters, thawed if frozen and cut in half or into thirds if large
½ handful parsley, finely chopped
4 fillet steaks, each 4-5cm/1½-2in thick
1 tablespoon chopped fresh chives or capers (optional)
Salt and ground black pepper

Carpetbag steak is basically a thick steak with a side pocket filled with oysters. I may be rash to claim the dish for Australia. James Beard says that different versions (sometimes called pocketbook steak) used to be in fashion in New Orleans and on the US West Coast. But Australia is a land of gastronomic indulgence, as anyone can tell you who's uncomfortably flipped through the Australian magazine *Vogue Entertaining* on a full stomach, so it's unsurprising to find carpetbag steak a popular party dish there. In London I make it now and then for private dinners when customers are mad for surf and turf. Despite using beef fillet, it works out a lot cheaper than steak with lobster. Frozen Japanese oysters really come into their own for this, as with other cooked oyster dishes, because they are convenient and economical.

Poaching the oysters before grilling the meat makes a version of carpetbag steak requiring the least work, but it's the least interesting tastewise, so I recommend chopping the oysters, rolling them in matzo crumbs and deepfrying them before stuffing the steak pocket, or serving either version with a Hollandaise or Béarnaise sauce. Or alternatively, my favourite method, which follows.

Combine the garlic purée with the butter in a small sauté pan and gently heat. Add the oysters and sauté them until they are lightly golden and beginning to turn crisp, then add most of the parsley and turn off the heat.

Using a sharp pointed knife, cut a big side pocket in each steak and fill with the fried oysters. Either chargrill the steaks, or pan-fry them on a cast iron skillet or frying pan that's nearly red hot. Dish up, spooning the remaining butter with garlic over each steak, sprinkling with the remaining parsley, and optionally adding some chives or capers. Season and serve.

If you are prepared to go totally mad, on the principle of form affinities you might accompany carpetbag steaks with soufflé potatoes – the deep-fried ones that magically puff up to look like little pillowcases – which are made as follows in the next recipe.

SOUFFLÉ POTATOES

4 large potatoes, old/mature
(which is important), of a
floury variety such as Maris
Piper
About 1 litre/1¾ pints rendered
suet, vegetable oil, or a
combination
Salt

Peel and cut potatoes lengthwise – another thing that matters – into uniform 0.3cm/⅛in slices (and classically, trim the slices into uniform rectangles or octagons), blotting them dry on both sides with kitchen paper. Cooking, a two-stage process, is best done in a deep sauté pan with a frying thermometer rather than in an electric frier. Stage one, heat the oil to 135°C/275°F, then drop in a small quantity of potato slices at a time, carefully agitating the pan back and forth to keep the floating slices bathed in fat. When they start to puff, or at least start looking semi-transparent, remove them and drain on fresh dry kitchen paper. Any puff showing at this stage will deflate while the slices cool off to room temperature.

Stage two, when ready to serve, heat the oil to 190°C/375°F, drop in the now cooled slices a few at a time, and again agitate the pan to keep the slices bathed in fat. Most of them will puff up immediately. You can either use the duds as chips with some other dish, or else put them aside, let them cool off again, and try frying them a third time at the end. The potato pillows should be fried until golden brown. Drain on kitchen paper, sprinkle with salt and serve them pronto.

SOUTH PACIFIC NON-CALORIFIC (SEAFOOD FRITTATA)

This different but delicious dish emerged after my husband said, 'Everyone loves frittatas. If you made one with an Antipodean spin, would that be *Il Postino* mixed with *Picnic at Hanging Rock?*' I pitched back: 'Could have shrimp. Something low-calorie; maybe Thai flavours.'

A frittata is an Italian omelette, though as with the tortilla or Spanish omelette, the eggs are usually the least of it. A great one can be made from leftover spaghetti with a filling of tomato, salami and cheese as a sort of egg-encased Spaghetti Bolognese.

For the frittata envelope:
2 shallots, thinly sliced
1 tablespoon olive oil
450g/1lb beansprouts
5 eggs, lightly beaten
Salt and ground black pepper
A drizzle of olive oil

For the filling:
165g/6oz cod or other white fish
    fillet
165g/6oz peeled shrimp
1½ tablespoons Cá Cóm fish
    sauce
1½ tablespoons garlic purée, or 1
    tablespoon chopped garlic
1½ tablespoons lemon juice
1 teaspoon grated lemon rind
    (zest)
Handful coriander, coarsely
    chopped
Salt and ground black pepper

For garnish:
4 large prawns, deveined, or 4
    crayfish
4 sprigs coriander
2 tablespoons salmon roe
    (optional)

Well, what emerged from our script conference *is* a lowish-calorie dish because it does without pasta and cheese, though some eggs and butter are necessary since it's a frittata. The crafty stroke – if I immodestly say so – is to use those usually gormless strands, beansprouts, as vegetable spaghetti, tuned up with some sautéed shallots and coriander. Cod and shrimp are likewise tuned up with stinky fish sauce: Cá Cóm from Bangkok, available at oriental grocers.

This dish superficially resembles other pub favourites by being made in the form of a cooked cake cut into wedges and served with garnish. It may just achieve the style and a vague recollection of Thai cooking without resorting to a single blade of lemon grass.

In a sauté pan, cook the shallots very slowly in the oil until soft. Put the shallots in a bowl with the beansprouts, eggs and seasoning, and mix together.

Poach the cod and shrimp in a little water for 3 minutes, then drain well. Flake the cod into a second bowl with the prawns, fish sauce, garlic, lemon juice and zest, coriander and seasoning.

In a wide, oiled casserole just big enough to hold all the ingredients, build the frittata in layers. Add half the onion, beansprout and egg mixture. Then the filling, not quite reaching the edge of the casserole. Finally, the other half of the onion, beansprout and egg mixture and the four prawns or crayfish as garnish. Put the uncovered casserole in the oven and cook at 175°C/350°F/Gas 4 for an hour.

Remove from the oven and allow the frittata to cool for about 10 minutes. Cut into wedges with a prawn or crayfish for each portion, and the additional garnish of a sprig each of fresh coriander, and optionally some salmon roe.

SYDNEY OPERA HOUSE SALAD

8-10 heads chicory (the white things originally from Belgium, confusingly known as endive in France and the USA)
4 hardboiled eggs, cut in half
110g/4oz pine nuts
4 tablespoons extra virgin olive oil
1 tablespoon walnut oil
1 tablespoon balsamic vinegar
1 tablespoon coarsely chopped parsley
150g/5oz fetta cheese, crumbled
Salt and ground black pepper

If *I* say it's Australian then don't argue with me, it's Australian, even if I simply made it up myself. However, this dish might also be filed under the sub-category of mimetic food, which children and other innocent folk of a poetic nature appreciate. (Order a salad, stay for a whole mimesis.)

Since chicory is a highly flavoured semi-bitter salad leaf, it stands up well to a full-flavoured dressing. The one I specify here combines good extra virgin olive oil, a little walnut oil, balsamic vinegar and fetta cheese. Believe me, less would be less.

Shortly before serving so the chicory doesn't discolour, trim the bases of all but two of the chicory heads, then cut them each in six wedge-shaped lengths the long way. The last two chicories should have their white shell leaves dissected individually.

Now build your Sydney Opera House on a big white plate, using chicory lengths and chicory shells with hardboiled eggs for support, finishing off with the individual chicory leaves as soaring forms. (You can hold things together with a few toothpicks if you want, but they'd better be the kind with frilly ruffs for visibility.)

Panfry the pine nuts in a dry pan until they are golden brown, then sprinkle them over the salad and between the chicory shells. For the dressing, combine the oils and vinegar, parsley, seasoning, and about two thirds of the fetta cheese in a jar and shake vigorously. When ready to serve, pour the dressing over the salad, mainly down among the lower leaves, and use the remaining third of fetta cheese as a garnish. Check for general structural integrity before presenting at table.

Sausage dishes inspired by U.S. diners and Eurobistros

The goodness of sausages isn't hot news. Everyone loves them, and there are dozens of authentic ways that meat pushed into casings can be dished up apart from Bangers, Mash and Onion Gravy (page 62). Here are just a few other ways I've served them.

Personally I don't like combining hot dogs with polenta, or Chinese sausages with sauerkraut – there must be reasons why each sausage nation developed its own serving notion. But I have no qualms about serving Italian, German, American and Chinese sausages on successive days, because when it comes to sausages, the English are ready to be the world's most cosmopolitan eaters: they just love them every which way.

HOT DOGS IN BUNS WITH AMERICAN MUSTARD AND SAUERKRAUT

12 US-style frankfurters
12 hot-dog buns, or bread rolls
    of similar shape and size with
    poppy seeds
250g/9oz prepared sauerkraut
American mustard, such as
    French's
250g/9oz tinned baked beans
    (optional)

Meatwise, frankfurters – known as hot dogs when served – can be anything from anywhere. Kosher (all beef) hot dogs and German-style franks can be OK. The ones I get are great, but my butcher has his own source. So if you fancy serving the most popular food item in the world, perennially enjoyed by American kids at base-ball games and birthday parties, I'd first check out the delicatessen section of a large enterprising supermarket. Go for anything labelled 'premium' hot dogs and avoid the cheap products.

Split the frankfurters the long way, leaving one edge hinged, then grill on both sides in a sizzling pan without any fat. Meanwhile, toast the split buns or rolls in the oven, in a suitable toaster or in another pan. Heat up the baked beans if serving them, but not the sauerkraut – Americans don't usually do that.

A genuine hot dog comes assembled with a generous wodge of sauerkraut on the toasted bun, then the hot dog split or unsplit, then the sugary mustard already in place on top (ketchup is bogus), all half-wrapped in a paper napkin. Baked beans are added on the paper plate alongside.

TOULOUSE SAUSAGES WITH DIJON MUSTARD AND SAUTÉED ONION POTATOES

8 Toulouse sausages (John's were a good 20 x 3cm/8 x 1½ in)
900g/2lb potatoes, any type, parboiled and peeled
225g/8oz onions, thinly sliced
150ml/5fl oz goose fat and vegetable oil, or a butter and vegetable oil combination
Lots of salt and ground black pepper
Dijon mustard

As I write, I'm between Toulouse sausages, those wonderful elements of a cassoulet that can be enjoyed on their own. Proper Toulouses are made of *very* coarsely chopped lean pork, hard back fat, sugar, salt, pepper and saltpetre, but of course every maker of Toulouses gives them his/her own *je ne sais quoi*. John, the butcher of Soho's Randall and Aubin, the maker of the best-tasting Toulouses I know, has moved to Fulham since the Brewer Street shop suddenly and sadly closed. He said on the phone he'd drop by and tell me how he made them, but so far no show. Still, it isn't much good knowing *how* to build sausages unless you're *prepared* to build them, which is a diabolical nuisance. Others still do make them and you may know where some good ones can be found. Let's take it from there.

Fat sausages like John's creations should first be poached, then panfried or grilled so the pork is thoroughly cooked. Half fill a frying pan with water and poach the sausages for six or seven minutes, turning once or twice. Pour off the water, reduce the heat, punch holes in them with a fork and slowly panfry them – again, turning a few times, for about ten minutes or until the sausages are well browned on all sides.

In another moderately sizzling pan, mix the potatoes and onions in the fat and oil. Add the seasoning, and carry on without turning too frequently until the mixture is slightly blackened. Serve together with a big dollop of Dijon mustard.

GERMAN SAUSAGES WITH GRAIN MUSTARD AND LENTILS / HOT SAUERKRAUT / WHITE RADISH

I confess I don't know as much about German sausages as I should, but then neither do most chefs, despite the fact that one of the greatest manifestations of French gastronomy, the brasserie, is basically a bistro with an Alsatian (i.e. Germanic) slant. German sausages are usually smooth-textured. I gather most are smoked, they usually contain a little saltpetre, and sometimes spices such as cumin (that's the knackwurst or knock-wurst), coriander and mace (that's the true frankfurter), or cinnamon, nutmeg and cloves. There is bockwurst, a mainly veal sausage seasoned with chives. Names like mettwurst, bratwurst and wieners have gone by me. I've probably eaten them without having been introduced. I apologise. But then I'm not telling you how to create them, just how to prepare them.

In the Munich beer hall where I once spent a pleasant afternoon, the litre steins of lager were accompanied on request with plates of sliced onion or plates of white radish cut into spirals (sausages and lots of other things were served in the dining room upstairs). White radishes are much larger, longer, and slightly milder than red ones. In Germany I bought a plastic screw gadget with an attached blade which I used for a while back in London to cut my own white radishes into spirals.

I shouldn't leave the subject of sausages from Mitteleuropa without dropping the names of Hungarian salami, the most delicious hard salami – it's perfect when eaten sliced up thinly in scrambled eggs, or simply on its own – and Polish kielbasa (the plural is kielbasy), the garlic and marjoram-flavoured pork and veal sausages, often ring-shaped, that come fresh or cured.

I won't give a list of ingredients or a how-to-do-it for this one, just a few more notes. German sausages have many mildly spicy flavours and appear in different colours. They usually come smoked and precooked, so they require only a few minutes heating up in a pan of water off the boil. I think they go perfectly with those grainy sweetish Meaux mustards that there aren't very many other uses for. So if you've received a jar from a gourmet aunt, here's the moment to break the red sealing wax and dig in. I also recommend the accompaniment of lentils (page 87), warm sauerkraut, and of course, thin slices if not spirals of white radish, which you may find are called mooli or daikon in the Asian shops and supermarkets where they are usually obtainable. A big boiled potato with a few flecks of parsley goes well alongside, according to custom in the beer halls of Bavaria.

CHINESE SAUSAGE SPINACH SALAD

110g/4oz white bread, diced
30ml/1fl oz vegetable oil
2 tablespoons garlic purée, or 4 garlic cloves, finely chopped
3 tablespoons sesame seeds
12 Chinese sausages, cut into long 1cm/½in diagonal slices
250g/9oz spinach, washed, spin-dried and trimmed with stems removed
2 tablespoons sesame oil
2 tablespoons unflavoured vegetable oil
1 tablespoon wine vinegar
Salt
Pinch of crushed dried chilli

Chinese sausages are available in packets in oriental supermarkets. They have a quite special sort of wry flavour that must be due to having been salted in unusual salts and then semi-dried. They're perfect for a snack with ironic friends. This dish in its original form was the very good suggestion of Fay Maschler.

In a frying pan, make garlic croûtons by browning the bread in the oil heated with the garlic. Drain them on kitchen paper, then add the sesame seeds to the pan and brown them slightly.

In a steamer, or a pan of boiling water with a strainer and a cover over that, steam the sausage slices for a few minutes until they are very hot and the fat is runny. Add the spinach in one or more batches and steam it for only a few seconds each batch so it just starts to wilt.

In a salad bowl, toss together the spinach, croûtons and sesame seeds, plus the mixture of sesame and vegetable oils, vinegar, salt and chilli. Scatter the Chinese sausage slices on top and serve.

Opposite:
Hot Dogs in Buns, page 45;
German sausages including
bratwurst (pale colour),
knackwurst (squat shape),
bockwurst (long and thin) and
Hungarian salami (slices), page
47; Lentils page 87; Chinese
Sausage Spinach Salad, page 48;
mug of Adnams Best Ale

SPICY ITALIAN SAUSAGES WITH COARSE TOMATO SAUCE AND POLENTA

12 or 16 spicy sausages
250g/9oz quick-cooking polenta
1½ teaspoons salt

For the sauce:
4 large garlic cloves, finely
    chopped
3 tablespoons olive oil
1kg/2¼lb tinned tomatoes
1 tablespoon balsamic vinegar
    (or Chinese black vinegar)
1 teaspoon salt
1 teaspoon sugar
Handful flat-leaf parsley,
    chopped
1 teaspoon crushed dried chilli

Like most sausage dishes where the sausages aren't homemade, this one comes down to good shopping. The shop is I. Camisa and Son Continental Provisions, 61 Old Compton Street, London W1, one of the Italian groceries I love in Soho (the other main one is Lina Stores in Brewer Street). Along with their fresh herbs, homemade pastas and special torte cheeses, Camisa sell their own wonderful coarse all-meat sausages, and they *are* wonderful: either spicy (peppery) or plain. I prefer the peppery ones and use them in this very modest but delicious and popular dish. In size the sausages are about 9cm/3½in long and 2.5cm/1in thick, so assume three per person or four per greedy person. If you are miles from London you can certainly make this dish with a local variety of sausage, but I assure you it won't be as good as Camisa's. Polenta, or maize meal, makes a delicious and authentic accompaniment. The pesto and tagliatelle option which follows this recipe is even simpler.

Prick the sausages and roast them on a rack in a 230°C/450°F/Gas 8 oven for about 20 minutes until cooked through and browned.

For the coarse tomato sauce, add the garlic to the hot oil. When it begins to brown, add tomatoes, vinegar, salt, sugar, most of the chopped parsley and the chilli, then simmer for half an hour.

The polenta quantity given here will serve four, but you might make up the whole package and let the remainder cool as the leftover is delicious later sliced and fried or grilled. In either case, boil 1 litre/1¾ pints water, or the amount specified on the packet, with the salt. Add the polenta and stir continuously for 5 to 10 minutes to prevent lumps.

Assemble the polenta on plates to form warm pools that will become squishy firm as they cool, sausages on top and plenty of coarse tomato sauce on the side. Add the remainder of the chopped parsley as garnish.

Left:
Scotch Eggs made with quail eggs, page 61; Pickled Eggs made with beetroot vinegar, page 115; Coleslaw, page 116

SPICY ITALIAN SAUSAGES WITH PESTO SAUCE AND TAGLIATELLE

12 spicy sausages
500g/18oz fresh tagliatelle
2 tablespoons pine nuts

For the pesto sauce:
170ml/6fl oz prepared pesto
  sauce *if ingredients are same
  as below* (at least one Italian
  brand is), or else chop
  together in a food processor:
150ml/5fl oz olive oil
2 tablespoons pine nuts
3 garlic cloves
45g/1½oz butter
1½ teaspoons salt
1½ large handfuls basil leaves
  (added just at the end)
90g/3oz Parmesan cheese, grated
  by hand (mixed in
  afterwards)

Prick the sausages and roast them on a rack in a 230°C/450°F/Gas 8 oven for about 20 minutes until cooked through and browned. Or poach them in a frying pan with water for 10 minutes, then pour off the water and panfry them for 10 minutes.

For the tagliatelle, bring a large pan of salted water to a rolling boil and then drop in the noodles. Start tasting after one or two minutes for al dente doneness; when done, drain into a colander, saving a few spoonfuls of hot water for the sauce. The pesto is a cinch if you are able to find one of the fugitive Italian brands that has all the right ingredients present and correct in the preparation, as one or two do (bring your reading glasses to the Italian grocer and read those labels). Otherwise, it's not difficult to make as described.

Serve it all up in a covered serving dish with the drained tagliatelle, pesto sauce, a couple of spoonfuls of hot water and the uncut whole sausages mixed together, with some extra pine nuts sprinkled on top.

2 THE ENGLISH PUB
TOP TEN

extraordinary versions of traditional dishes

Mooney's Bar

SHEPHERD'S PIE / COTTAGE PIE

3 tablespoons vegetable oil, plus a little extra for the pan
675g/1½lb best lean minced beef
2 onions, finely chopped
Salt and ground black pepper
2 teaspoons ground mace
120ml/4fl oz leftover gravy, meat glaze, or water with a dissolved beef stock cube
225g/8oz carrots, diced or coarsely grated
½ handful parsley, chopped
225g/8oz marrow peas, may be tinned or frozen
450g/1lb potatoes, boiled, peeled and mashed with swede
450g/1lb swede, peeled, boiled and mashed with potato
30g/1oz butter, diced while cold

When I first began running pubs and cooking for pub customers, my mother back in Australia (a superb cook, if my daughterly observation can be deemed reliable) asked what kind of food I did. I mentioned shepherd's pie. 'Ah, Pom food,' she said. Her remark wasn't intolerance, but an amiable acknowledgement that shepherd's pie and cottage pie have international fame. It's most likely because of what the dishes have in common: piecrusts based on mashed potato rather than pastry.

To deal with shepherd's pie first. As its name betokens, it's essentially a minced lamb dish, though other meats are often mixed in. My friend Beth Coventry makes a super version. In addition to the main ingredients of minced lamb, onions, milk and potatoes, Beth also includes cinnamon, mint, celery, carrots, tinned tomatoes, Gruyère cheese, bacon and olive oil.[7]

Myself, I generally make cottage pie. Leftover lamb is fiction in a pub, and when I need to order minced something-or-other from the butcher it's nearly always lean beef I ask for. My recipe is way simpler than Beth's, though the slightly novel crust mixture of swede and potato seems to add a bit of rigour to what can become a sentimentally undisciplined dish (and I do mean *sloppy*). Try to contrive that your cottage pie can be served up with a knife and fork like a pie, not with a ladle like a stew. Coleslaw (page 116) makes a good accompaniment.

Lightly oil a sauté pan and fry the minced beef gently for a few moments, stirring frequently, then pour off the rendered fat and reserve the meat. Put the 3 tablespoons vegetable oil and onions into the pan and sauté until the onions are soft. Combine the onions with the minced beef and then add salt, pepper, mace, the gravy or other liquid and the carrots. Cover the pan and simmer over low heat until the carrots are soft and most of the liquid has disappeared. Stir in the parsley and peas, correct seasoning if necessary, then put the mixture into a casserole.

If you have a pastry bag with a large rosette tip and don't

---

7 Don't hesitate to try winging it from the ingredients mentioned, but if you're too timid a cook, Beth's recipe gets a full writeup on pages 100-101 of Elizabeth Jane Howard and Fay Maschler, *Howard & Maschler on Food*, London 1987.

mind washing it up afterwards, it's the best way to apply the combined mashed potato and swede, because the frilly edges of squeezed-on mash will brown beautifully and decoratively in the oven. Otherwise, spread on the mash with a fork and try to achieve a similar frilly effect. Dot the mashed topping with bits of butter and bake at 200°C/400°F/Gas 6 for about half an hour, when the topping will have become two tones of brown and cream.

FISH PIE

450g/1lb cod, filleted
450g/1lb whole scallops
225g/8oz button mushrooms, finely sliced
55g/2oz butter
45g/1½oz plain flour
110g/4oz petits pois
2 egg yolks
170ml/6fl oz single cream
Salt and ground black pepper
1 tablespoon lemon juice
55g/2oz Gruyère cheese, grated
1 packet frozen puff pastry

For the court bouillon:
280ml/10fl oz white wine
560ml/20fl oz fish stock, (could be made with Ikan Bilis granules)
1 bay leaf
10 peppercorns
2 sticks celery
½ handful parsley

There are Pom food versions (see my comments in the introduction to the previous recipe) of fish pie that use mashed potato piecrusts. Nothing wrong with them. I once made them regularly myself with Nick Reader, my very able cook at The Unicorn, later my Three Greyhounds barman. This is a slightly more sophisticated pastry version that's come down life's fishpike since. For a *less* sophisticated fish mélange that lacks any sort of crust, *see* Coley Jumbo on page 100.

Use four oval pie dishes for this, about 14cm/5½in long – the glazed earthenware kind, usually with a rim – since the pies will be runny.

First bring all the ingredients for the court bouillon to the boil, then simmer, covered, for 20 minutes. Add the cod, scallops and mushrooms and continue simmering for five minutes, then remove the solids with a slotted spoon. Turn up the heat and bring the stock to a rolling boil without a lid, reducing the liquid by a third.

Melt the butter in a sauté pan, stir in the flour to make a roux, then slowly add the reduced stock, stirring constantly, to thicken it. Beat the egg yolks with the cream into a froth and stir into the sauce. Add seasoning and lemon juice, then the fish, flaking any big pieces, the mushrooms and peas, and stir together. Pour the mixture into the pie dishes and sprinkle the grated cheese over the surfaces. Roll out enough pastry to make a 0.3 cm/⅛in thick piecrust lid for each, crimping round the pie dish edges. Bake at 200°C/400°F/Gas 6 for 20 minutes.

CHILLI

Tarantula Jack's ingredients:
- 1.3kg/3lb top sirloin, cut into very small cubes (around ⅛in [0.3cm] square)
- 2 medium Spanish onions, grated or coarsely chopped
- 2 large cloves garlic, minced
- 560ml/20fl oz chicken broth
- 400ml/14fl oz Hunt's tomato sauce (or Italian plum tomatoes)
- 7 tablespoons mild chili powder
- 2 tablespoons ground cumin
- ¼ teaspoon cayenne pepper

Chilli (or chili, the Tex-Mex spelling) is a great example of gastronomy on the move. As far as I can discover it started as a Mexican dish of no great renown, Chile con Carne, which is stewed, spiced minced meat with tomatoes. The confirmation of its origin is its equally delicious but less versatile Mexican sibling, Chile con Queso – runny spiced cheese with tomatoes. Like many Mexican dishes, chilli moved north across the border and began a transformation.

The first transformation was a strong association with beans. According to James Beard, the authority on American cookery, many variations of 'Southwestern Chili Beans' have come from Arizona, Nevada and New Mexico, and a dish Beard called 'Cowpuncher Beans' combines both meat and beans with the chilli and tomato. Since the mid-1980s, chilli has become a great favourite in the best of London pubs, where the recipe is essentially similar to Cowpuncher Beans. At the Conniving Weasel, a chilli would be unthinkable without both the meat and the beans. Before giving my own recipe, however, I should note that since Beard's day America has gone into ever more refined versions, where cooks again eschew the beans.

For instance, Tarantula Jack, winner of the 1991 World Chili Cook-off held in the USA, won that contest by enhancing a plain dish to a high desert mesa of finesse. American opinions are sure definite on chilli: 'cumin should be the only identifiable spice,' said one expert at the cook-off (as reported by Richard Erlich in *The Guardian*). Fieryness is a defect, and the quality of the chilli powder is important. Chilli should be not too wet nor too dry: 'halfway between sauce and stew'. Rice is held to be the proper side dish, though some prefer hominy grits. Jack's recipe, and wording, for making his prizewinning 'Thundering Herd Buffalo Tail Chili' is as follows:

'Sauté beef in frying pan. Put it in your favorite chili pan and simmer with the onions, garlic and broth for 1½ hours. Keep your nose out of it and keep the lid on! Add the tomato sauce and chili powder and the ground cumin. Stir. Let this cook on low for another 1 hr 15 mins. Add water as needed. After 2 hrs 45 mins, take the lid off and enjoy the aroma of the greatest chili ever to slide into a bowl. Add the cayenne pepper and put the lid back on and simmer for another 15 minutes. Time for a great bowl of red!'

MY CHILLI

My ingredients:
2 Spanish onions, coarsely chopped
Vegetable oil
Chilli powder
1 whole head of garlic, finely chopped
2 tablespoons tomato purée
3 tablespoons vegetable oil
900g/2lb lean minced beef
Ground mace
Bay leaf
1 or 2 400g/14oz tins tomatoes
1 or 2 400g/14oz tins cooked red kidney beans
Leftover wine or beer (optional)
Salt

Like many pub dishes, this is best cooked the day before and reheated. I serve it with hot rolls and green salad.

Sauté the onions in vegetable oil until soft. Judging the age/strength of the chilli powder, add enough to the oil so the dish will be quite fiery. Add the garlic, tomato purée and the beef in small batches, browning and stirring with the onions and spice. Give a liberal sprinkling of ground mace and salt. Add the bay leaf and tomatoes. If you have some leftover wine or beer, put it into the pot. Allow to stew, adding the red kidney beans five minutes before the conclusion. What you want to finish off with is a very piquant red-coloured thick stew of minced beef and undisintegrated beans.

LASAGNE

For the meat sauce:
4 tablespoons butter and olive oil mixture
1½ tablespoons onion, finely chopped
1½ tablespoons celery, very finely chopped
1½ tablespoons carrot, very finely chopped
225g/8oz lean beef, minced
Salt
170ml/6fl oz white wine
110ml/3½fl oz milk
Ground black pepper
Ground nutmeg
280ml/10fl oz tinned tomatoes, chopped

For the pasta:
340g/¾lb commercial fresh lasagne pasta, or homemade from ingredients as follows:
3 eggs, small
270g/10oz plain durum flour
¾ teaspoon salt

For the béchamel sauce:
1 500ml/18fl oz container prepared Chef Bechamel, or homemade as follows:
55g/2oz butter
1 tablespoon flour
500ml/18fl oz milk
1 onion studded with 3 or 4 cloves
1 bay leaf
250ml/9fl oz chicken stock
Salt
Butter, for greasing the baking tin
110g/4oz parmesan cheese freshly grated

In my opinion, my Lasagne con le Verdure or Vegetable Lasagne on page 129, is gastronomically superior to the meat version, but then...(a mumbled coarse remark about what it would take to turn the Queen into the King). In other words meat lasagne is King, deserving or not: as seen on a pub blackboard menu, many customers are drawn. Apart from its filling, the methods are pretty similar. My meat filling is adapted from Marcella Hazan's superb *The Classic Italian Cookbook*.[8]

Just a few words about ready-made béchamel sauce. I almost never use manufactured sauces because of their cost, especially at the pub where it might be a question of 20 portions. Exceptionally (as I say for the ingredients of Sour Onion Tart), I sometimes use a few drops of Maggi because of its unique taste. Another exception, applicable for this dish, is Chef Bechamel, put up by the Italian company Parmalat in 500ml/18fl oz cardboard containers; it contains nothing other than ready-cooked whole milk, cream, flour, corn starch and salt, so it's practically *comme il faut*, and when I use it I cut it with some stock so it doesn't really end up as packaged. I get it from Lina Stores in Soho, who also sell lasagne pasta freshly made (as some supermarkets now do). This dish can't be done well with dry pasta.

For the meat sauce, in a heavy based saucepan swizzle the onion, celery and carrot gently in the butter and oil until the onion is soft, then go on sautéing for a minute more. Add the beef and ½ tablespoon salt and fork the meat apart until it is browned. Add the wine and turn up the heat to evaporate it all, then turn down the heat to a simmer, add the milk, pepper and nutmeg, and cook while stirring until the milk has evaporated. Add the tomatoes, stir, turn down the heat to the least possible simmer, and cook uncovered for 3 ½ hours, stirring occasionally.

For homemade pasta, combine the eggs with as much flour as they will take without becoming dry or crumbly and the salt, then knead by hand for about 8 or 10 minutes until elastic and smooth, then stretch it out very thinly to improve elasticity, then

8 New York, 1976.

ball it up again. With a rolling pin, roll it out to about 0.3cm/⅛in thickness.

For homemade béchamel sauce, melt the butter over low heat and blend in the flour. Stir in the milk slowly, adding the onion and bay leaf, and simmer while whisking until it thickens. Remove the onion and bay leaf. For ready-made sauce, warm it up. Add the chicken stock and a little salt.

A rectangular baking tin is orthodox for lasagne, but I prefer a round one to make a lasagne for four. Don't blanch the pasta first. Grease the tin with butter then layer the sheets of pasta and meat sauce alternatively starting and ending with pasta – for a *minceur* version, three pasta layers, for a *gourmande* version, four. Add a little béchamel sauce and grated cheese at each level, and finally pour béchamel sauce on top in a nonchalant manner and let it find its way down. Sprinkle the remainder of the cheese (that is, most of it) on top. Bake on the hottest upper-most level of the oven at 230°C/450°F/Gas 8 for 15 to 20 minutes maximum. Allow to cool for a few minutes before serving.

STEAK AND KIDNEY PIE

225g/8oz veal, beef or lamb
 kidneys
45g/1½oz kidney suet, made up
 with butter if necessary
1 onion, chopped
450g/1lb stewing steak, trimmed
 of fat and cut into 2.5cm/1in
 cubes
½ handful parsley, chopped
400ml/14fl oz beef stock
 (optionally including some
 lager or Guinness)
Salt and ground black pepper
1 tablespoon Worcestershire
 sauce
2 tablespoons Madeira or port
2 tablespoons flour
1 packet frozen puff pastry

Let's roll up our sleeves and get quickly down to business on this famous British dish. It's a top-crust-only pie that can be done in a single open casserole or glazed pie bowl, or in four individual glazed pie dishes – the oval sort with rims that are about 14cm/5½in long. The kidneys and their suet rightly provide the gastronomic occasion, but I notice that readymade pies that come in tins often lack kidneys, and some customers fish out the kidney chunks and leave them by the side of their plates. Steak and kidney pies aren't generally served with anything else but a glass of brown ale or cold lager.

Clean the kidneys as follows: remove the outside membrane. Split large veal or beef kidneys lengthwise and remove the white fibre and fat from the centres; this is not necessary for lamb kidneys. Save all suet for the recipe. Soak the beef kidneys (not the veal or lamb) in vinegary water for an hour. Drain, blot dry and cut into 1.5cm/½in cubes.

Melt the suet and any butter in a sauté pan. Add the onion and sauté until soft. Add the steak and brown it all over, then add the parsley, stock, seasoning, Worcestershire sauce and Madeira and simmer for about 1½ hours.

Add the kidneys, then slowly stir in the flour, stirring constantly. For superior pastry, allow the filling to cool before putting it in the casserole or pie dishes. Roll out enough pastry for a thickness of about 0.3cm/⅛in and cover the casserole or dishes. Bake in a 220°C/425°F/Gas 7 oven for an hour or a bit more, until the crusts are golden.

BUBBLE AND SQUEAK

8 medium or 6 large potatoes, boiled, peeled and coarsely chopped (half of that volume or less could be similarly prepared turnips)

2 large onions, chopped, or better, same amount of chopped shallots

4 tablespoons butter plus oil, or better – chicken dripping, or ideally – goose fat left over from the Christmas goose

Salt and ground black pepper

½ Savoy cabbage, finely sliced

55g/2oz pancetta or bacon, diced (optional)

2 tablespoons caraway seeds

4 or 8 eggs

8 or 12 slices black pudding

Two onomatopoeic words together make a lovely onomatopoeic name for a dish. Bubbles rise from between curds of fat-fried squashed potatoes. The squeak is from cooked cabbage. (Colcannon, the fashionable Irish version, is generally made with shredded Brussels sprouts.) The flavours are delicious too. As for provenance, I suspect this traditional English fare began as an all vegetable family dish made from leftovers that included carrots and turnips or what-had-they, much loved by the children of creative frugal cooks. This elegant version is a homage and also a slight transformation. Ingredients are cooked fresh, and the caraway seeds give it an added Mitteleuropa touch.

Boil the potatoes until partly cooked, then peel and chop them. Sauté the onions or shallots in fat until soft. Add the potatoes, salt, and lots of pepper. Allow to brown on the bottom, then break them up and turn them over, repeating, until lots of coarse brown crusts are intermingled amid the white potato curds.

Meanwhile, blanch the cabbage in boiling water. Mix the cabbage with the potato mixture in the pan, and add caraway seeds and cooked pancetta or bacon, if using. Adjust the seasoning, allow to sit (this is yet another dish which is rather better the next day) and reheat when ready. Serve with slices of grilled black pudding and one fried egg each, or two for the greedy, atop each portion. If black pudding does accompany the Bubble and Squeak, pancetta or bacon isn't really necessary.

BEEF STEW: A DUMB DAUBE

900g/2lb stewing beef, trimmed
  of fat and cubed
225g/8oz belly of pork, cubed
110ml/3½fl oz olive oil
5 shallots, peeled
10 small garlic cloves
12 small round pickling onions,
  peeled
450g/1lb carrots, scraped and cut
  into chunky rounds
½ handful parsley, chopped
6 sprigs fresh thyme, or 1
  teaspoon dried thyme
1 bay leaf
225g/8oz black olives, stoned
Salt and ground black pepper
Red wine to cover (allow a bottle
  or slightly more)

As I said (on page 33) when discussing what to do with wine ends, daubes are quite simple. The reason is that, unlike some other stews, the ingredients aren't precooked separately to achieve different flavours or textures, they all blend together. So I won't apologise for the simplicity of mine. In fact, that is why I think of it as a dumb daube.

If you fancy serving this in jellied slices cold, include a calf's foot in the pan at the beginning, or stir into the liquid two packets of gelatine at the end of the cooking according to the packet instructions. Hot or cold, this is excellent with boiled potatoes.

In a sauté pan, swizzle the meats in the olive oil until they are browned. Transfer them to a casserole or stewpot with the remaining ingredients and cover with the wine. Put on the lid and cook in a 175°C/350°F/Gas 4 oven for 4 hours.

SCOTCH EGGS

For the forcemeat:
1kg/2¼lb lean veal
500ml/18fl oz chicken stock, or
    water and stock cube
6 anchovy fillets in oil
2 raw eggs
1 handful parsley
Salt and ground black pepper
3 tablespoons capers, chopped if
    large
Small amount of breadcrumbs
    (optional)

12 fresh free-range chicken eggs,
    or 36 quail's eggs
1 egg, beaten, for dipping
170g/6oz matzo meal
Groundnut or sunflower oil for
    deepfrying

Almost universally, pubs buy Scotch eggs in catering packs. They are made from battery eggs boiled so hard they are greenish around the yolk, then coated with heavily rusked pork sausage meat. Next they are dipped in breadcrumbs containing poisonous-looking orange food colouring, and finally deepfried in a nameless hydrogenated oil. Sound attractive?

Because customer expectation about Scotch eggs is so low, I usually leave them well alone to be served at other places in their typical horrid form. But once in a while I sentimentally think that, since Scotch eggs are a great pub standard snack, they ought to be done . . . not as they used to be; I can't prove they ever were . . . but as they could be. Perhaps they should be called Edinburgh eggs. Or Charles Rennie Mackintosh eggs.

Whatever one might call them, this way of doing them is delicious. They make a perfect snack for picnics, cocktail time, or watching football. Beth Coventry and I once did the quail's egg version for a luncheon party of chefs, and we got a round of applause, because chefs love new wrinkles on tired classics.

For the forcemeat, trim off any veal fat, coarsely chop the veal then poach in the simmering stock for 5-10 minutes, and drain, reserving the stock for another dish. Put the veal, anchovies, 2 raw eggs, most of the parsley, and salt and pepper (slightly over-season, for the benefit of the eggs to come as well) in a food processor and process until finely chopped. Add the capers afterwards, with some breadcrumbs if you want to use them.

Put the chicken or quail's eggs in a pan, cover with cold water and bring to the boiling point. The quail's eggs will then be cooked, so plunge them into cold water. The chicken eggs will need simmering for 6-8 minutes before being plunged into cold water. Shell the eggs and coat them thickly with the forcemeat. Dip them in the egg binder and then the matzo meal, then deep-fry the eggs a few at a time in 190°C/375°F oil until the crumb coating is brown.

The old pub way of serving is a plain cold Scotch egg on a plate; a nicer way is to serve either the chicken or quail's egg version cut into slices on a piece of buttered toast. Garnish with the remaining parsley.

BANGERS, MASH AND ONION GRAVY

This is the full-plate version of the basic British fast food. A few words first, however, on each of the ingredients.

The bangers: many newspapers and television food programmes do reports evaluating Britain's best sausages. Of course the real issues are not finding out where they come from in Yorkshire or Devon, but whether you can get hold of them easily and, notwithstanding the Oscars, whether you and your guests will like them when you do. I've concluded that sausages are an enormously personal taste, not necessarily related to advisory standards, gastronomic awards or even healthy ingredients. Personally I can't stand sausages loaded with fat and rusk – give me a great Toulouse sausage every time, or at least a mostly-meat British one – but some people I hugely respect do love them. My conclusion is that you should buy what your family or guests like, and not be unduly impressed by the awards. If you're stumped, make a start by going to Sainsbury's or Tesco's and trying their 'premium' sausages. You know that sausages aren't very good for the cardiovascular system wherever they're from, so I suggest not having them more than once a week!

The mash: there are numerous ways to do satisfying mashed potatoes. It really depends on what they're accompanying. There's nothing like the taste of the mashed potatoes that stuff a goose, but unless you've saved up some goose fat, you may as well forget that one. And it would be silly to accompany bangers with one of those mashed potato jobs full of cream. So how? For choice, use a variety of floury, mealy potatoes like King Edward, Maris Peer or Maris Piper and boil them whole in their skins so they don't disintegrate. Once a fork reveals them to be tender, drain them, cut them in half and, after letting them begin to cool for a couple of minutes, start peeling. If you let the peeled potatoes stand quietly on your worktop for a couple of minutes longer a lot of unnecessary water will steam off. Mash the potatoes with some butter, and optionally, hot milk. (I confess I never use the latter but lots of great mashmakers do.) A superhint is that after being *mashed*, really superior mashed potatoes should be *whisked* with a balloon whisk or even a fork. Delia Smith mashes and whisks simultaneously with an electric whisk. Don't forget the salt.

The onion gravy: this is the tough part. Unless you already have some surplus gravy, how do you produce something that doesn't taste like reconstituted gravy granules? Well, you'd better be aware for a start that many people actually like the taste of reconstituted gravy granules. Ignoring them, I'd proceed by building up a worthwhile onion and liquid base, and then trying to achieve the right flavour without sinking heavily into the hands of monosodium glutamate and friends. My method is to slowly stew lots of finely sliced red onions in butter and oil until they are very soft but not brown. Add red wine ends for the liquid and reduce that by about a third (which of course evaporates the alcohol, too), then add a knob of butter plus half of a premium (as the supermarkets say) beef cube, such as Knorr, and any further seasoning necessary. If thickening is desirable, as it probably would be with bangers and mash, I do it with the traditional butter-and-flour mixture, a spoonful of each, making a roux to which the oniony liquid is slowly added in a pan. And of course, I add to all of that any leftover gravy.

To prepare, just mash the potatoes. Concoct the gravy. Grill the sausages. And if you've never actually seen bangers, mash and gravy, The Movie, there is nothing fancy about the presentation. It looks like two sausages side by side, a mound of mashed potato next to them, and a pool of gravy next to that (not on it).

FISH AND CHIPS

For the batter:
1 egg
280ml/10fl oz lager
150ml/5fl oz milk
250g/9oz plain flour mixed with
     55g/2oz potato flour

1kg/2¼lb good frying potatoes,
     such as Maris Piper or
     Desirée, peeled, cut to about
     1 x 1 x 5cm/½ x ½ x 2in (if you
     want a rough target size),
     and temporarily put in a bowl
     of cold water
At least 2 litres/3½ pints
     groundnut, corn, or other
     vegetable oil
4 fillets of cod, haddock or plaice
50g/2oz plain flour seasoned
     with salt and black pepper
Salt and ground black pepper
Malt vinegar (and/or lemon
     slices, or tomato ketchup) to
     serve

While fish and chips is unquestionably in the English Top Ten of all-time food favourites, I may be accused of stretching a point by calling it one of the English Pub *Top Ten* because pubs don't often serve it. In justification, *I* do. Achieving fish and chips in a pub (or at home) isn't so easy, but here's how to go about it.

The first thing you want – in the fish-and-chip *feinschmecker* phrase – is 'a nice piece of fish': cod, haddock and plaice are the traditional ones the English prefer to batter and fry. Then, you want a light batter: I'm suggesting one. For the chips, the well-known secret is to fry them twice (you can see how it's done by watching at MacDonald's or Burger King). Finally, you want to possess either an electric deep-fat fryer, a frying thermometer, or a good sense of temperature.

First, mix the batter ingredients together and refrigerate for half an hour. Next, prepare the potatoes, then heat the oil to 150°C/300°F. Fry the chips in batches for the first-stage cooking for 5 or 6 minutes (when they will not yet be browned). Drain these in a wire basket or on kitchen paper.

Start to raise the temperature of the oil to about 185°C/360°F. Dredge the fish fillets in flour on both sides, dip them in the batter, and fry them in the oil until the batter has puffed and become a rich golden orange. Remove and drain as with the potatoes. Finally, finish off the chips in the oil for 2 or 3 minutes until they are golden brown. Drain, season, then serve with vinegar, lemon or ketchup.

3 HARKENING BACK WITTINGLY

The Lounge at the Warrington

FIRE ISLAND GASPACHO

225-340ml/8-12fl oz tomato juice
2 green peppers, seeded but
 unpeeled
4 tomatoes, scalded and peeled
3-5 garlic cloves, peeled
1 stick celery
1 large cucumber
1 or 2 eggs
55ml/2fl oz olive oil
110ml/3½fl oz vinegar
Salt and a pinch of cayenne
 pepper

For the garnishes:
1 green or red pepper, seeded
 and finely chopped
2 eggs, hard-boiled and either
 coarsely chopped or pushed
 through a sieve
1 onion, finely chopped

Soups aren't standard menu items in pubs, but often are for pub private parties. And of course gaspacho is a great summer dish: cold, raw, and so healthy. Because gaspacho could be subtitled 'What You Will', there's no reason to detain you with anything but a superior version. This, which makes the finest gaspacho I've tasted, is a recipe my husband collected on Fire Island, New York, in 1965.

Normally I have real antipathy for green peppers, those android vegetables. When I come across slices of them in salads they seem unpleasant and quasidigestible. But that fault has a compensating virtue. Their jaunty, plasticky crispness survives even a blender, so their texture and slightly *X Files* taste are fundamental to this recipe. Even if you generally concur with my view, cast prejudice aside and use them.

Blend together in small amounts, using a bit of tomato juice with each batch, the peppers, tomatoes, garlic, celery, cucumber and raw eggs. Put this in a container that can be chilled. Add olive oil, vinegar, enough further tomato juice for a thick but liquid consistency, salt and some cayenne pepper. Chill until very cold and the flavours have had a chance to mix. Serve with the cold garnishes in separate dishes.

HAM HOCKS (PORK KNUCKLES), SPLIT PEA SOUP

2 ham hocks, sometimes called pork knuckles (the elbow-to-wrist front leg joints; one feeds two), salt-cured like gammon, not smoked
1 onion stuck with 2 cloves
1 tablespoon caraway seeds
2 bay leaves
1 tablespoon sugar
170ml/6fl oz malt vinegar
8 carrots, trimmed and sliced into lengthwise quarters
900g/2lb waxy potatoes, peeled unless skins are finely smooth

The two parts of the heading are separated by a comma rather than 'and' because ham hocks (sometimes called pork knuckles) and split pea soup are parts of different meals. As soup and main dish for the same meal they would seem a bit indistinct, so I've planned for the soup to begin after the ham hock has had its day. Maybe recipe books don't usually do this but real-life cooks have to consider combinations and plan the further use of unexhausted ingredients all the time. That is, nothing here is a 'leftover'. All you have to do is save the remains of the ham hock in the fridge to make the soup some time later, after the earlier taste has receded from the memory.

Cover the knuckles with water in a stockpot and boil for five minutes. Then turn off the heat and skim the top of the liquid. Add other ingredients, apart from the carrots and potatoes, and simmer, covered, for an hour. Add the carrots and potatoes and simmer for a further 20-30 minutes until they are tender.

Carve the ham hocks on a serving plate. Serve accompanied by al dente Savoy cabbage, and a sauce made from a little reduced stewing liquid combined with Dijon mustard. After the meal, reserve the remaining meat and bones from the ham hocks in the stewing liquid (separating any leftover potatoes or cabbage) and refrigerate.

500g/18oz split peas
Stewing liquid from cooking the ham hocks, fat removed after refrigeration
Ham hock meat (see recipe above)

Split Pea Soup
Rinse the split peas under running water in a sieve. Taste the stewing liquid and if it tastes strong, combine the washed split peas in a pan with a small proportion of it, reserving the rest, and making up the liquid in the pan with plain water to about 2 litres/3½ pints. Simmer for about 1½ hours and taste. If the flavour now seems too strong, add more water; if too weak, add more of the reserved stewing liquid. Finally, slice up the remaining ham hock meat and add to the soup, warm through, correct the seasoning, and serve.

TOAD-IN-THE-HOLE WITH ONION GRAVY

8 cooked English sausages or small Toulouse sausages, nicked with a knife and torn into careless-looking jagged slices
Dripping or butter for greasing bowls or pan

For the reduced-fat Yorkshire pudding mixture:
250g/9oz *plain* white flour, not self-raising
¾ teaspoon salt
310ml/11fl oz skim milk
3 eggs

For the onion gravy:
4 red onions, thinly sliced
2 tablespoons vegetable oil, butter, or a combination
Salt and ground black pepper
1 teaspoon Worcestershire sauce
110ml/3½fl oz wine, beer or vinegar
110ml/3½fl oz homemade beef or chicken stock
1 tablespoon butter
3 tablespoons flour – or instead of the stock, butter and flour, 110ml/3½fl oz water, plus gravy granules with thickener

To demystify the jokey English name, this is simply sausages in Yorkshire pudding. I make Toad-in-the-Hole in individual oven-proof bowls, served alongside onion gravy, accompanied by English mustard and tomato ketchup. For four, you may prefer making it in a square baking pan and turning out the toad-in-the-hole in four pieces, with a bit left over for the greedy.

While the sausages are grilling or frying, put the ovenproof bowls or the roasting pan in the oven and heat up to 230°C/450°F/Gas 8. Assemble the Yorkshire pudding ingredients in a mixing bowl and give them a desultory stir-through, not worrying about the odd lump which will disappear while baking (beating until fluffy not only isn't necessary, it militates against a good semi-soggy result. We want pudding, not a loaf of bread). Take the hot bowls or pan out of the oven and wipe the insides with kitchen paper containing dripping or butter. Put the sausage slices in bowls or pan, then pour the Yorkshire pudding mixture over them (the sausage won't stay at the bottom) and pop back into the oven.

Meanwhile, for the onion gravy, sauté the onion in the oil or butter until soft, then add salt, pepper, Worcestershire sauce, the wine, beer or vinegar, and beef or chicken stock if you are using it. Bring to the boil and reduce by about a third. (If you are using gravy granules, reduce the liquid after you have added the wine, then stir in the water and granules.) If you are using homemade stock, thicken it with a roux: melt the butter in a small saucepan, add the flour and stir both together for a few minutes, then add the onion mixture spoonful by spoonful to the roux until all of it is absorbed.

The Toad-in-the-Hole will be ready in 20 or 25 minutes. Check by looking. It should look semi-raised and semi-soggy, neither wet and raw nor dry and hard. The onion gravy is served alongside it, not on it.

CORNED BEEF HASH AND FRIED EGGS

500g/1lb 2oz potatoes, peeled
   and cut into 1cm/½in dice
2 large white onions, chopped
340g/12oz (one tin) corned beef
45g/1½oz beef dripping (best),
   butter (second best) or 3
   tablespoons vegetable oil
1 tablespoon Worcestershire
   sauce
½ teaspoon ground mace or
   fresh grated nutmeg
Salt and cayenne pepper
Flat-leaf parsley, as garnish

For the fried eggs:
8 very fresh eggs
1½ teaspoons butter
Salt and ground black pepper

If you duck into Annabel's in Berkeley Square in London to escape the nightingale uproar you may be surprised to see this homely dish on their menu, which their chef does (or at least used to do) wonderfully. There are a million wrong ways and one right way to do it. Here it is, more or less.

Boil the potatoes until they are about two minutes underdone, then mix together the onion, the potatoes and the corned beef flaked from the tin. Since the final crusting stage is helped by having the ingredients start cold, you might put the mixture in the fridge for a few hours, or add small splashes of cold water to the hot pan at judiciously chosen crusting moments later, or else not be bothered to do either.

Fifteen minutes before the food is to be served, melt the dripping in a heavy frying pan and add the hash mixture, pressing it down and sizzling it relatively slowly. When the hash crusts in the fat, scrape it up in spatula-sized slices and turn over. Repeat this many times, adding the Worcestershire sauce, either mace or nutmeg, and seasoning.

Start to fry the eggs towards the end by melting the butter in another clean heavy pan. When the butter starts to sizzle, reduce the heat and add four eggs – four more in a second batch. Their yolks will put up with a lot before breaking if they are very fresh. (If they aren't so fresh, it's better to poach them.) While frying, baste the yolks with melted butter from the pan and add salt and pepper. Cut eggs apart in the pan with a sharp knife before attempting to lift them with a spatula.

The hash will be ready when there is a *substantial* amount of dark brown crust flecking all through it, and a good dark, but not black, crust on the bottom. Whatever you do, don't skimp the crust or undercook, because unmelted fat in the hash is disagreeable – the idea is to make the corned beef's fat and jelly join the general sizzle, which is what makes mere corned beef become delicious.

When ready, the hash should be turned out crusty side up and either brought to the table alongside the fried eggs on a serving platter, or divided on to large individual plates partnered by two eggs each. The traditional garnish is a little flat-leaf parsley, and the traditional accompaniment is a bottled chilli sauce, such as Tabasco.

ROAST BEEF HASH

75g/2¾oz beef dripping, augmented with butter and vegetable oil if necessary
2 onions, chopped
340g/12oz potatoes, peeled and coarsely chopped
600g/22oz roast beef and roast beef fat, diced
Salt and ground black pepper
8 or 10 long sprigs fresh thyme, chopped, or 1½ teaspoons dried thyme
Handful parsley, chopped
Poached eggs, to serve (optional)

Though roast beef hash is a champion dish, I make it far less often than corned beef hash. Roast beef sandwiches are great sellers, and my butcher would never send me a roast beef so negligently trimmed that bits of it weren't good enough for my sandwiches. What *is* 'leftover roast beef' anyway? It is largesse probably only to be found around the Double Q Lazy B cookhouse, or at the barbecue alongside the bullring in Chihuahua. If you ever find yourself stuck with some, though, you can prepare a taste even more exceptional than corned beef hash. While CBH has flavour that largely depends on its salty cure, RBH's flavour comes from the holy union of beef, onion, parsley and thyme. If you like the taste of beef as found in steak tartare, you will certainly love roast beef hash, its cooked cousin.

Melt the dripping and sauté the onions in it until they are transparent. Add the potatoes and sauté gently until they begin to brown, then add the beef. At first turn the mixture over a lot with a spatula, but when the potatoes are nearly cooked stop poking around so much and let the mixture begin to crust up. (The addition of cream at this stage will form a heavy crust as well as add lots more cholesterol, but I prefer the flavours without it.) Add salt, pepper and the thyme.

When about ready, the dish will be very brown and crusted, and, of course, the beef will be very well done – one of the exceptional occasions when well-done beef is wonderful. While the hash is still on the heat a moment before serving, add the parsley and turn over some crusty slices with the spatula so the parsley is worked in a bit. Serve the roast beef hash with poached eggs if desired (a good idea), and put on the table a bottled chilli sauce.

OXTAIL STEW

55g/2oz suet, butter or vegetable oil
2 large or 3 medium onions, chopped
1½-2½ tablespoons tomato purée
1 tablespoon mild paprika
2 oxtails, chopped into sections by the butcher
55g/2oz flour seasoned with salt, black pepper and paprika
1 teaspoon celery seeds, or 1 rounded teaspoon celery salt
1 orange spiked with 10 cloves
2 bay leaves
Salt and ground black pepper
8 carrots, trimmed and split lengthwise
½ handful parsley, chopped

For the mashed potatoes:
8 mealy potatoes, boiled
55g/2oz butter
Salt and ground white pepper

This is a real ragoût, as its defining liquid becomes naturally thickened by the gelatine in the oxtail. If Guinness is Good For You, having a plate of oxtail stew with it should certainly set you up for a month. Should its liquid be made from stock and/or wine, as some hold? I think that with oxtail as the protagonist, stock is unnecessary; wine, which is pretty expensive in Britain, should be saved for recipes where it makes a difference. The celery seeds, orange and clove refinements below are my mother's effective subtleties.

Preferably the day before the oxtail is to be eaten, melt the suet in a sauté pan and swizzle in it the onions, tomato purée and paprika. Put the oxtails in a plastic bag with the seasoned flour and shake, then add them to the pan and brown them with the onion mixture, adding the celery seeds or celery salt. Barely cover the meat with water, add the orange and the bay leaves, then cover the pan and simmer for two hours. Cool, chill, and the next day take off the fat (or skim off the fat while warm if making the dish the same day).

Add the seasoning and carrots to the stew and simmer for another hour. Meanwhile, boil the potatoes separately. Mash them and whip with the butter, seasoning and some of the parsley.

Remove the meat and carrots from the stew and discard the orange and bay leaves, then reduce the liquid for a few minutes over high heat. If it needs further thickening, whisk in a paste made from some of the liquid and some seasoned flour. Put the meat, carrots and liquid in a serving dish. Serve with the mashed potatoes and fresh chopped parsley.

CELTIC STEW

Mutton or lamb bones
1 onion stuck with 2 cloves
1 bay leaf
2-3 large garlic cloves
2 sprigs thyme
½ handful parsley, chopped
Salt and ground black pepper
1.5kg/3lb 6oz shoulder of mutton
 by preference – or lamb,
 boned, trimmed of fat and
 cut in large cubes
110g/4oz onions, sliced
2 leeks split, washed and diced
500g/18oz potatoes, peeled and
 sliced
500g/18oz turnips, unpeeled and
 diced
2 carrots, sliced and cooked, as
 garnish

For the caper sauce:
30g/1oz butter
2 tablespoons flour
280ml/10fl oz mutton stock
Salt and ground black pepper
10-12 grinds of nutmeg
110g/4oz capers, chopped if large

The Connaught Hotel restaurant, I believe, does Irish stew as a classic menu item. I haven't eaten it there to become influenced by it, so this is my own version. It's been touched with several elements of a Scottish national dish (gigot with turnip including that wonderful accompaniment, caper sauce), which turns it into a sort of Celtic stew. Even my Italian customers like it though.

Traditionally, Irish stew used mutton, and strong flavour came readymade with the meat rather than with gastronomic methods and blandishments. While lamb wouldn't be a distressing substitution, I think if you want to do this dish you should go for it rather than turn out something a bit too delicate. Ask your butcher if he can supply you with mutton shoulder; otherwise try a Halal butcher. Have the butcher bone the shoulder and give you the bones as well. These quantities should serve six to eight.

First make some mutton stock, preferably the day before: add mutton bones, onion, bay leaf, garlic, thyme, half the parsley, some salt and pepper to about 2 litres/3½ pints water in a stockpot and bring to the boil. After a few minutes skim off the scum, reduce the heat, and simmer for 2 or 3 hours. Either carefully pour off practically all the fat while hot, or – better – chill the stock and remove the fat when it has become solid.

For the caper sauce, make a velouté sauce with butter and flour by heating them slowly in a double boiler and gradually whisking in a portion of mutton stock. Simmer the thickened stock for about an hour with an occasional stir, then correct the seasoning and add the nutmeg and capers.

Now for the stew proper. Put the mutton pieces in a flameproof casserole or heavy-based pan with the onions and leeks. Cover ingredients with mutton stock and simmer. After an hour, taste a piece of mutton for tenderness and give it 20 minutes more if it needs it. When the meat is sufficiently tender, add the potatoes and turnips and cook for a final 20-30 minutes until they are also tender. Correct the seasoning and add the rest of the parsley. Serve with just a few spoonfuls of liquid per portion, garnish with the sliced carrots, and spoon the caper sauce either alongside on each plate or serve it in a sauceboat on the table.

TRIPE LYONNAISE

675g/1½lb red onions, chopped
3 tablespoons unfancy olive oil
1 tablespoon tomato purée
3 tablespoons sherry vinegar
About 1 tablespoon homemade
   meat glaze, or a beef stock
   cube
1kg/2¼lb white prepared
   honeycomb tripe, rinsed if
   necessary, then cut into strips
   of about 7.5 x 0.5cm/3 x ¼in
   strips
2 handfuls parsley, chopped
Salt and ground black pepper
1kg/2¼lb floury potatoes, boiled,
   peeled, mashed and whipped
   with butter and seasoning

Yet another flavoursome favourite to be eaten with mashed pota-toes and accompanied by a glass of Burgundy or a cold lager. Tripe Lyonnaise makes me think of where I grew up, far from Lyon in a suburb of Sydney, because it was a frequent Saturday night dish of my mother's. Prepared tripe is the muscle of beef or ox stomach, scraped, soaked in lime solution, rescraped, partly boiled and vinegared; the tenderer 'honeycomb' tripe comes from the second stomach that ruminants have. This recipe is for brown French tripe; not white English boiled tripe and onions, a dish mostly loathed ('Ugh – not tripe, Mum'), though loved by a minority.

Gently sauté the onions in oil until soft, then add the tomato purée and swizzle. Next comes the sherry vinegar (lacking that, use red wine or distilled vinegar, *not* malt or balsamic), plus a strictly unthreatening amount of homemade meat glaze or beef cube because the flavours will intensify while cooking, and finally the tripe strips plus half the chopped parsley.

Barely simmer for an hour in the covered pan, then correct the seasoning. Serve the tripe either alongside a mound of mashed potatoes if you are artistically diffident, or in a sculpted volcano of mashed potato if you aren't – with a sprinkling of chopped parsley as make-believe volcanic ash.

CHINATOWN SPARE RIBS

2 racks pork spare ribs (the 'American' cut of short ribs)
3 tablespoons vegetable oil
3 onions, roughly chopped
1 tin (400g/14oz) *condensed* beef consommé
1 tablespoon soy sauce
1 tablespoon honey or marmalade, or more, to taste
2-4 garlic cloves, finely chopped
1 tablespoon freshly grated root ginger
2 tablespoons Dijon mustard or tomato ketchup
1 teaspoon Worcestershire or Tabasco sauce
110ml/3½fl oz red wine (optional)
2 tablespoons Hoi sin sauce (optional)
Salt and ground black pepper
Chinese plum sauce, to serve

Fay Maschler was determined to crack the secret of pork spare ribs the Chinese restaurant way, and didn't rest until she had done it. An elaborated report of her recipe was first printed in the London *Evening Standard* in the days when she was responsible for their cookery column as well as restaurant criticism, and later appeared in her collection *Eating In* (1987). This is a version from about five years earlier which she gave to a friend over the phone. It's slightly different, but it contains the secret ingredient tinned condensed beef consommé, and the essential advice to turn the sauce into glue ('enamel' was the more *soigné* word she later used in print). Two racks of spare ribs will serve four over-generously perhaps, but this recipe requires too much prep to be worth bothering with in any smaller amount. Warm sauerkraut goes with it a treat.

Cut apart the ribs and arrange them with as much exposure in one layer as possible in one or more large baking tins, covering them with foil. Roast for 25 minutes in a very hot oven, about 230°C/450°F/Gas 8 or higher, to render off all the fat you can.

While the rib fat is being rendered off, sauté the onions in oil in a pan until very brown (the caramel will brown and flavour everything), then add all other ingredients to the pan and boil to reduce the liquid by about a third. This is powerful stuff on its own, but it won't seem that way on the ribs.

Remove the rib pans from the oven, discard the foil and pour off the liquid fat. Coat the partly cooked ribs in the pan or pans with the reduced sauce. Roast for about an hour, starting at high heat and reducing it later or the ribs may end up charred. Baste with the sauce frequently. The ribs are ready when they look dark brown and chewy and the sauce is a gummy glue sticking all over every rib. The orthodox accompaniment, as a dip in a side bowl, is prepared Chinese plum sauce from an oriental supermarket.

STUFFED CABBAGE LAYERS

1 dark green Savoy cabbage,
    divided into leaves
30g/1oz onion, chopped
3 tablespoons olive oil
90g/3oz butter
30g/1oz celery, finely chopped
30g/1oz carrot, grated or
    chopped
340g/12oz minced pork
150g/5½oz chicken livers,
    coarsely chopped
2 teaspoons salt and ground
    black pepper
225ml/8fl oz dry white wine
110ml/4fl oz milk
Grated nutmeg
450g/1lb tinned plum tomatoes
    with juice, roughly chopped
4 slices brown or wholemeal
    bread, crumbed

The predictable boiled-vegetability of stuffed cabbage adapts to any provenance, like sitcom. Sometimes it's great, sometimes you only think of boiled cabbage. There is an American version, resembling Greek minced lamb in stuffed vine leaves, which is done with minced pork in rolled and skewered cabbage leaves. There is a Middle Eastern Jewish aromatic version made with whole, cored heads of green cabbage stuffed with minced beef, rice, cumin and turmeric. The Polish version is sweet-and-sour. And then there's my version, different from all the above; though, of course, it seems rather familiar, harkening back wittingly. Like sitcom.

Blanch the cabbage leaves for a few minutes, drain them and reserve. Make a ragù of the other ingredients as follows: sauté the onion in oil and butter until soft, add celery and carrot and cook for 2 minutes, add the ground pork, forking it in with the vegetables, add chicken livers and the salt, and then sauté until the meats are barely brown. Add the wine, turn up the heat, and cook until all the wine has evaporated. Turn down the heat, add the milk and nutmeg, and cook, stirring frequently, until the milk has evaporated. Finally, stir in the tomatoes. When they start to bubble, turn down the heat, cover, and cook at a bare simmer for at least 2 hours.

Assemble the stuffed cabbage layers in a buttered deep baking dish, as for lasagne, alternating layers of cabbage leaves and ragù. Cover the top with breadcrumbs and a few bits of butter. Bake for 1 hour in a 160°C/325°F/Gas 3 oven. If you want to make the dish even richer it could be doused in béchamel sauce exactly like lasagne, but without that it's lighter, and I think goes better with a pint of ale.

CALF'S LIVER AND BACON WITH POTATOES

500g/18oz potatoes (see method)

250g/9oz sweet-cured streaky bacon, thinly sliced and rinded if necessary

6 very thin slices calf's liver (includes 2 extra for the greedy)

110g/4oz flour seasoned with salt and ground black pepper

30g/1oz butter and 2 tablespoons vegetable oil

Chopped parsley, as garnish

I only have two things to say about this: (1) thin-liver-very-hot-skillet, and (2) forget about onions – they're in the wrong flavour region, in my opinion.

Start with the potatoes: if you are using New, boil them; if they are a floury type, mash them with butter; or make sautéed potatoes – the Hash Brown version on page 107 is good. Keep them warm in the oven.

Next, separate the bacon slices and panfry them until they are nearly crisp; pour off the bacon fat and reserve. Blot the bacon on kitchen paper, then keep the slices warm on a large serving platter in the oven.

Either scrub and polish the same frying pan, or use a fresh one for the liver. Lay out the liver slices and dredge with seasoned flour on both sides. Heat some of the butter, oil and bacon fat in the frying pan. When the fat is almost smoking, give each slice of liver, in turn, about 20 seconds for each side: move on to the next when each looks like it's covered with mocha powder (scarcely browned) on the outside because if your liver is as thin as it should be, it will then still be pinky red inside. Add more butter, oil and bacon fat to the pan as necessary. The livers join the bacon on the big platter in the oven, basted with the remaining butter and bacon fat. When all's ready they get dished up with the potatoes, and garnished with chopped parsley.

NOISETTES OF LAMB WITH LEMON AND GARLIC RELISH

675-900g/1½-2lb lamb in the form of rolled loin, rolled shoulder, loin chop or slices of leg

1 tablespoon garlic purée, or a heaped teaspoon of crushed garlic

500g/18oz tortiglioni or large fusilli – if tomato-coloured pasta is available, it makes an agreeable colour

30g/1oz butter

For the relish:

½ tablespoon grated lemon rind (zest)

1 tablespoon finely chopped garlic

3 tablespoons finely chopped parsley

1 tablespoon lemon juice

About 3 tablespoons olive oil

Salt and ground black pepper

A noisette is either a hazelnut or a small lamb or mutton steak. My catering butcher does noisettes from a loin of lamb that he fillets, then reverses, rolling in the long comma of flesh. He then wraps and ties it in a thin cylinder of its own fat – a very elegant piece of meat. The apparent reason for the name is that when it is roasted and sliced at a bit of an angle, the otherwise roundish medallions become elliptically nut-shaped. However, my suggested accompaniments work equally well with other lamb cuts such as roasted boned and rolled shoulder, chargrilled loin chop or even pan-fried slices of leg. Lamb is a wonderfully natural, unmessed-about and delicious meat, and this way to serve it is a slightly different alternative to the usual way with integrally larded splinters of garlic and rosemary.

The accompanying lemon and garlic relish is closely related to gremolada, an Italian garnish usually served with osso bucco (braised veal shanks). Its traditional form is very pungent, so my version is a weedier sister: without a herbal combination, and cut with oil and some lemon juice. As well as being excellent with lamb, it's quite delicious when mixed with a slightly chewy fresh pasta shape like tortiglioni or fusilli (both corkscrews), so I suggest the addition of one of those to complete the dish.

Rub the lamb all over with garlic purée, then depending on its form and your fancy, either roast it whole, chargrill it, or panfry the slices until browned on the outside and still pink inside.

While roasting/grilling/frying, combine ingredients for the relish, using only enough oil to make a quite stiff mixture that will settle slowly into a pool. Put the pasta in boiling water and cook until al dente, then drain and toss with butter and salt and pepper. (Grated parmesan is not recommended with the lemon tastes of the relish.) Serve on plates holding noisette-y slices of lamb to the left, a crescent of pasta to the right and a mound of relish in the middle.

QUICHE LORRAINE

2 bacon rashers, rinded and
    finely chopped
1 shallot, finely chopped
15g/½oz butter
3 eggs
225ml/8fl oz single cream
    (preferable), or milk
110g/4oz Gruyère cheese, grated
30g/1oz Parmesan cheese, grated
½ handful parsley, chopped
Salt and ground black pepper

For the shortcrust pastry:
90g/3oz butter, at room
    temperature
165g/6oz plain flour

Quiches were a popular lunchtime dish in the '60s and '70s, then suddenly had naff appeal. About the time that every lady caterer began to supply quiches for directors' lunches with a stalk of asparagus on each slice, the jokes started. Even a book, *Real Men Don't Eat Quiche*, appeared. The popularity temporarily ebbed... then returned powerfully for a spring tide as commercially made ones started to appear in pubs, angled at vegetarians: big unappealing wedges of 'egg pie' with dark flecks of courgettes and mushrooms. Oh no (sadly), no.

Even if the stodgy courgette and mushroom version is the only sort you are familiar with, put prejudice behind you. Make a quiche as it was made when the world was young. We are talking about the genuine, original, delicious one. Quiche Lorraine. My version includes some cheese.

You need a 25cm/10in tart tin with removable bottom and fluted edges. For the pastry, rub the butter into the flour, dribble in some cold water, and knead, but don't knead too much – bits of unintegrated butter don't matter. Put the dough in the freezer for up to an hour so it doesn't soften when rolled out. Roll out the dough to about 0.3cm/⅛in thick and use to line the tin. Insert greaseproof paper and weigh it down with dry beans or the like. Bake in a 200°C/400°F/Gas 6 oven for 10 minutes. Remove the paper and beans, prick the pastry liner and bake for a further 3 minutes.

While the blind-baked pastry case is cooling, sweat the chopped bacon and shallot in the butter until the bits of shallot are soft. Distribute the bacon and shallot in the pastry case. Whisk together the eggs, cream, cheese, chopped parsley and seasoning and pour the mixture over the bacon and shallots. Bake at 190°C/375°F/Gas 5 for 25 minutes, then cool for 5 minutes. Pop the bottom of the pan upwards to release the quiche, which may be served either hot or at room temperature.

SALADE NIÇOISE

1 small red onion, thinly sliced
    into rings
4-5 small ripe tomatoes,
    quartered
340-400g/12-14oz fine green
    Kenya beans, cooked until
    crisp-tender
225g/8oz potatoes, cooked and
    coarsely sliced
3-4 hardboiled eggs, coarsely
    chopped
200-300g/7-10oz tuna in oil (1 or
    1½ tins)
6 anchovy fillets
55g/2oz stoned black olives, or
    green Spanish olives stuffed
    with anchovy
10-12 large fresh basil leaves, cut
    into a chiffonade

For the dressing:
3-4 large garlic cloves
1 sundried tomato
1 anchovy fillet
1 teaspoon balsamic vinegar
Juice of ½ lemon
About 120ml/4fl oz extra virgin
    olive oil
Salt and ground black pepper
2 tablespoons prepared
    mayonnaise (optional)

Unlike a Caesar salad, which requires a dead literal pursuit of the proper form or else don't bother, salades Niçoise can be all over the place, and are. My excuse for including a recipe is to give the form that I serve and prefer. For a start, I ignore *Larousse Gastronomique's* dogmatic view that cucumber and broad beans should be in, potatoes and cooked vegetables should stay out, because I've been to Nice. In numerous bistros there, this classic salad is often made up approximately as follows.

Combine the salad ingredients, flaking the tuna but otherwise not tossing much or the soft elements will become mushy. Chop and churn the dressing in your herb mincer, or hand-mince and shake up in a bottle, then dribble all over the salad. The optional addition of prepared mayo may sound dubious, but its effect on flavour is negligible, while its integral vegetable emulsifier guarantees a reassuringly creamy coating on the salad.

HOUSE TERRINE

1kg/2¼lb veal, finely minced
250g/9oz belly of pork, coarsely minced
250g/9oz pork liver, minced or finely chopped
100g/3½oz firm pork fat, diced
5 garlic cloves, finely chopped
1 teaspoon crushed or ground mace
1 tablespoon juniper berries, semi-crushed
90g/3oz pistachio nuts
Salt and ground black pepper
Butter or lard for greasing the terrine
Bay leaves, as garnish (optional)
Thin bacon rashers, as garnish (optional)

A champion dish for serving cold in slices with a chunk of good bread alongside a simple salad with vinaigrette. See also Four-Meat Loaf (page 26) which can be served that way, and the chicken liver pâté recipe following.

Commercial pâtés sometimes have onions and eggs added, with a layer of aspic containing Jurassic-looking things on top, but in my view a good homemade one doesn't need such touches – even the pistachio nuts that I specify are borderline, though they look OK and add good flavour. The quantities make more terrine than four people require since it's silly to take the trouble for just a small amount. Try to get the textures of the different ingredients to vary, more or less as indicated.

Combine all ingredients except the butter or lard, bay leaves and bacon rashers, and knead together with your hands. To check the seasoning, fry up a spoonful and taste because to bring out all the flavour may take more salt than you think (a low-salt pâté is a contradiction in terrines!).

Grease either a suitably sized rectangular metal tin or an elegant casserole with butter or lard, then fill with the mixture and garnish with bacon and/or bay leaves. Cover with metal foil and bake in a 150°C/300°F/Gas 2 oven for an hour, then remove the foil and continue baking for another 1-1½ hours.

The terrine will shrink. Cool it under a weight to spread it against the sides again, unless your casserole is so elegant and the terrine looks so lovely it precludes that. Refrigerate.

CHICKEN LIVER PÂTÉ

250g/9oz chicken livers, trimmed and any discoloured bits discarded
250g/9oz butter
½ teaspoon ground mace
Salt and ground black pepper

Easy and very rich, this is simply a half-and-half mixture of butter and chicken livers. There's no garlic, cream, egg, or booze.

Sauté the chicken livers briefly in a little butter until the outsides look brown but the insides are still very pink. Melt the rest of the butter and add to the livers with the mace and seasoning. Blend into a purée, pour into a mould and refrigerate.

TUNA NOODLE SALAD

500g/18oz dried macaroni
5 or 6 celery sticks
200-300g/7-11oz tuna in oil (1 or 1½ tins)
2 teaspoons celery seed
Prepared mayonnaise
2 tablespoons extra virgin olive oil
Salt and ground black pepper

This bears some resemblance to Kedgeree 1 (page 91), my father's Sunday night tea special that our family loved, because both dishes combine carbohydrates and fat with tuna. This one was what my husband kept *his* children happy with when *they* were small, so the resemblance is familial as well as gastronomic. It's quick to do, laughably easy, and truly 'moreish' – that horrible word genuinely applies for once.

To explain some of the ingredients, the celery seeds bump up the dish's celery flavour without overcrisping its texture with too much actual celery. I've suggested the use of commercial mayonnaise because homemade mayo would go largely unnoticed alongside the robust tuna and celery taste. Just add a bit of full-flavour olive oil to the stuff that comes out of the jar. These quantities serve four generously.

Cook the macaroni for the time specified on the packet, then drain and rinse in cold water to bring it almost to room temperature. Chop enough thinnish slices of celery to make a volume about half as much as the cooked macaroni. Flake the tuna with a fork and add the celery seed. Combine all the ingredients and stir in enough mayonnaise to barely coat everything like thin enamel, then add the olive oil and the seasoning. Serve immediately at room temperature (best), or chill and serve (good).

Fowl and accompaniments

CHICKEN, LEEK AND HAM PIE

1.5kg/3lb 6oz free-range chicken ('free range' noticeably adds to the flavour)
1 litre/1¾ pints homemade chicken stock (ditto that on that 'homemade')
4 leeks
1½ handfuls parsley
55g/2oz polenta
250g/9oz good cooked gammon or ham, sliced in thin strips
Salt and ground black pepper

For the shortcrust pastry crust:
55g/2oz butter
110g/4oz plain flour
1 teaspoon salt
2 tablespoons iced water

I wouldn't be at all surprised to find that the combination of chicken and ham is one of the bashfully unassertive British gastronomic inventions. After all, chicken and ham together are also to be found in the cold pies you buy in English country pubs, as well as in the better version at Fortnum & Mason. This recipe has the addition of leeks, which is the very symbol of part of Britain (aren't they on the Welsh pound coins?), so it's practically time to sing 'Land of Hope and Glory'. And if I'm pretty ignorant about gastronomic history, maybe the recipe makes up for it. The addition of polenta as a quick, easy gravy thickener is my small contribution to the tradition.

Start by making the pastry in the food processor using the butter, plain flour and salt, and a dribble of iced water. Chill it.

Slowly poach the chicken in simmering stock, turning the chicken once or twice if the stock doesn't cover. While the chicken is simmering, wash and finely chop the leeks and chop the parsley, and reserve. After about an hour remove the chicken from the pan, allow it to cool a little to be able to handle it, then strip off all the meat from the bones. Reserve the meat.

Make the stock into gravy by adding the polenta slowly while stirring (the polenta will thicken it, giving the gravy a grainy consistency rather than a velvety one).

Fill a casserole or metal pie tin with the chicken and the strips of ham and top up with the gravy, then add the uncooked leeks and parsley – they will cook during the hour in the oven – and adjust the seasoning. If there is time to let the pie filling cool somewhat before baking it will make the baked crust better, but it will still be OK if not. Roll out the chilled pastry and fit over the top of the casserole or pie tin. Bake for one hour at 175°C/350°F/Gas 4. Remove the pie from the oven and allow it to cool for at least 15 minutes before slicing and serving.

GILDED PHEASANT

1 litre/1¾ pints chicken stock, homemade if possible
3 tablespoons unfancy olive oil
4 shallots, finely chopped
4 garlic cloves, finely chopped
2 pheasants, cocks by preference, cleaned and cut in half along the breast and back with poultry shears, giblets reserved
Salt and ground black pepper
1 tablespoon tomato purée, or 3 sundried tomatoes, finely chopped
1 tablespoon juniper berries, crushed
3 sprigs fresh thyme, or ½ teaspoon dried thyme
150ml/6fl oz red wine (optional)
300g/10oz black pudding with butter for frying (optional)
Parsley, roughly chopped, as garnish

'Gilding' is the word M. Denis Constant of Meyragues in the Bouches-de-Rhône used when he taught me this method, which I guess was a translation of *embellir* rather than *dorer* – at this juncture I prefer a slight mystery rather than precise knowledge. What it refers to is a two-stage cooking process of first stewing for tenderness, then roasting for golden crispness (though as you'll see, my version is actually three-stage: browning, stewing, roasting). It's especially appropriate for meat that would turn out tough if simply roasted, like the wood pigeon in the next recipe that gets a different form of gilding. For pheasant, it's mainly a delicious way of preparing it. And as I greatly prefer quite fresh pheasant without the gamy flavours that develop during hanging, the staged gilding process sidesteps any of the stringiness that could come from implacable freshness. To this dish I usually add my favourite accompaniment, black pudding.

Bring the chicken stock to a simmer in a stockpot and reserve. Heat the oil in a heavy sauté pan and add shallots and cook them until they are soft, then add the garlic. Turn up the heat and add the pheasant halves with salt and pepper. When the pheasant skins are beginning to turn golden brown, add the tomato purée, juniper berries, thyme and red wine if using. Stir around for a moment, evaporating the alcohol if there is any. Turn off the heat, then add to the stock the pheasants and other ingredients, scraping the bottom of the pan. Add the finely chopped giblets. Don't dilute the stock to make up more – if the liquid isn't quite enough to cover the pheasant halves (and it oughtn't to be), turn the pieces under the liquid three or four times while cooking. Barely simmer for an hour with the pot half covered.

Transfer the pheasant halves to the oven to 'gild' the skin for 25 minutes at 175°C/350°F/Gas 4. Meanwhile, boil the stock in the pan to reduce it by half to make a gravy, and panfry the black pudding (if using) in a bit of butter. Serve each half pheasant with plain brown rice, a garnish of roughly chopped parsley, and the gravy including bits of vegetable and giblet.

83

WOOD PIGEON

4 wood pigeons, cleaned and split in half along the breast and back with a knife or poultry shears, giblets reserved
1-1½ litres/1¾-2¾ pints chicken or game bird stock, homemade if possible
Salt and ground black pepper
30g/1oz butter, melted (optional)
Juice of ½ lemon (optional)

For many game-lovers, the prince of birds and flavour leader is grouse. My own preference is for wood pigeon. The meat is delicious, and it comes already portion-controlled because one pigeon is perfect for one person. Then there is that fulsome dark breast; pigeons are famous for their breasts. There's only one problem with wood pigeon. If you just roast it, the breast flesh hardens up like a Michelin tyre. The right thing to do is poach it, then gild it, which utterly solves the toughness problem. The most agreeable way is poaching in stock, then chargrilling.

What about accompaniment? It's best to serve pigeon (like most game birds) with a carbohydrate that will help hold the juice, such as a large croûton of toasted granary bread, bulghur, brown rice, wild rice, mashed potatoes, purée of celeriac and potatoes, or potato kugel; plus an earthy brown or dark green vegetable, such as green lentils, puréed lentils, puréed sprouts, puréed chestnuts, puréed artichokes (I'm rather big on puréeing), red cabbage. Or if you fancy, partner the pigeon with a single in-between vegetable that's carbohydratey and rather earthy at the same time, such as roasted parsnips or puréed broad beans.

Below, I suggest four alternative accompaniments. Three of them are quick, easy and delicious; one, potato kugel, isn't so quick, but is still easy and delicious. Further notes about them follow.

Lightly poach the wood pigeons in the simmering chicken stock for 5-6 minutes. Remove and reserve the stock for another dish or another occasion. Gild (or brown) the poached wood pigeons either by chargrilling them, lightly panfrying them in butter with a little lemon juice, or roasting them for about 12 minutes at 200°C/400°F/Gas 6.

Finely chop the giblets and either add to about 300ml/11fl oz of the stock and reduce to make a gravy, or add them to the accompanying dish of bulghur, lentils, or puréed artichoke.

BULGHUR

2 tablespoons goose fat (ideal), chicken dripping, or butter and vegetable oil combined
1 large onion, chopped
400g/14oz bulghur
2 tablespoons sunflower seeds (optional)
1-1½ litres/1¾-2¾ pints chicken stock, either homemade or made with water and a chicken stock cube
Salt and ground black pepper
200g/7oz pasta seashells or bowties (optional)

I think bulghur (which is to say cracked wheat) made this way is a better carbohydrate dish than bread pudding or couscous, and it's a perfect accompaniment for any poultry. Incidentally, the Russian dish kasha can be prepared in exactly the same way, though I don't think it's quite as delicious or versatile. Kasha is buckwheat groats.

Melt the fat in a large sauté pan, then cook the onion until it is soft. Add the dry bulghur and the sunflower seeds if using them, and stir all around until the grains are heated and thoroughly mixed with the fat and onion. Reduce the heat, then slowly add a little of the chicken stock, letting it simmer and be soaked up by the bulghur. Continue adding liquid until the bulghur is risotto-like in consistency, i.e. fat and moist but still chewy, and won't absorb any more: about 15 minutes of simmering should finish it off and cook it.

If pasta seashells or bowties are desired – which almost turns the bulghur into a main dish – cook them separately until al dente, then drain them and mix with the bulghur before serving.

POTATO KUGEL (POTATO CAKE)

4-5 potatoes, peeled
1 onion
2½ crushed matzos (matzos that you mill yourself will be slightly coarser and have better texture than packaged matzo meal)
2 eggs, beaten
2 teaspoons salt
½ teaspoon ground black pepper
Either 3 tablespoons vegetable oil, *or* 200ml/7fl oz beer
1 teaspoon baking powder
Chicken dripping (preferred), or butter, for greasing the baking pan

This is a Jewish family dish, but like many good gastronomic ideas it deserves liberation from the ethnic. Once or twice in the past I've probably told customers it was Irish Potato Diddly. Perhaps the original version with oil should be called 'Kugel' and the version with my novel substitution of beer (which gives it a slightly nuttier taste) should be called 'Diddly'. It's delicious either hot or cold.

Grate the potatoes on the fine grating disc of a food processor and reserve, then replace the grating disc with the steel blade and process all the other ingredients. If you intend to use beer in the mixture, first wring some water out of the grated potato in a clean tea towel before combining. Then hand-mix the grated potatoes with the other ingredients.

Pour into a well-greased casserole or pan and bake at 190°C/375°F/Gas 5 for about an hour, until the top is quite brown. Allow to cool slightly, then slice into rectangles or wedges for serving.

LENTILS

450g/1lb dried green lentils, or grey lentilles de Puy
400ml/14fl oz chicken stock, homemade, or water with a dissolved chicken stock cube
½ onion, chopped
1 bay leaf
1 dried bouquet garni (one 'teabag')
1 stick of celery, finely chopped
3 slices pancetta or sweet cured bacon, finely chopped
55g/2oz sunflower seeds
Salt and ground black pepper
4-6 tablespoons olive oil
2-3 tablespoons garlic purée

A lot of foolish oversoaking of lentils is going on. After much experimentation, here is my best result. This makes more than enough for four – more like enough for six. There's no point in making only a little.

Rinse the lentils under running water in a strainer, then soak in cold chicken stock for no more than half an hour. Add the onion, bay leaf, bouquet garni, celery and bacon. Bring just to the boil and immediately turn off the heat. Allow the lentils to stand in the liquid for a further half an hour to an hour, then taste. The lentils at this stage should be slightly undercooked, but almost tender.

Add a bit more liquid if necessary, the sunflower seeds, salt and pepper, and simmer for *a maximum* of 10-15 minutes more – otherwise the lentils will get too soft – tasting every couple of minutes to check the texture.

When serving, add a tablespoonful of olive oil and a few squeezes of garlic purée to each portion and stir. The uncooked garlic purée gives the lentils a wonderful floral taste. The lentils should be served warm, not hot.

PURÉED ARTICHOKE

Wood pigeon livers, if available, sautéd in 30g/1oz butter

12-16 tinned artichoke *bottoms*, or the bottoms cut from fresh artichokes and simmered for 40 minutes in water with a bay leaf, celery, and several crushed garlic cloves

2-3 garlic cloves (if using tinned bottoms)

½ teaspoon celery seeds (if using tinned bottoms)

15g/½oz butter

Juice of ½ lemon

1 fresh green bay leaf (if available)

200ml/7fl oz white wine and/or wood pigeon stock

Salt and ground black pepper

To finish:
Extra butter or lemon juice
Chopped parsley, to garnish

This is adapted from a wood pigeon recipe by Elizabeth David called 'Les Palombes à la Béarnaise'. As possible substitutes for globe artichokes, she suggests broad beans or Jerusalem artichokes. While broad beans are good, they are a little bland; Jerusalem artichokes are also good but famously farty, so go for the globe artichokes. My own modest innovation comes from having noticed that globe artichoke bottoms can be bought in tins. I don't mean artichoke hearts but artichoke *bottoms*, as they are actually called on the label. If you can manage to find them in a supermarket or speciality grocer, you have taken three steps to heaven. Unlike frozen Japanese oysters – q.v. my Oyster Stew– this particular convenience food comes very slightly at the expense of flavour, so the tinned version needs to be bumped up with garlic and celery seeds; fresh artichoke bottoms don't, since as I say, you should poach them with garlic and celery in the first place.

If pigeon livers are available, sauté them in butter and reserve. In a food processor, purée the artichoke bottoms with all other ingredients (including the sautéed livers if available, and a single fresh green bay leaf), adding the wine and/or stock to the mixture at the finish in just sufficient quantity so it becomes a purée rather than a cake or a soup. Adjust the seasoning.

Half fill a decorative buttered casserole with it, and to quote Ms David, 'put the pigeons on top of the purée and heat it gently'. Five minutes before the dish comes out of the oven, baste the pigeons with the extra butter or lemon juice and sprinkle with chopped parsley.

CHICKEN TARRAGON

4 chicken suprêmes (see introduction)
1 tablespoon vegetable oil and 1 tablespoon butter
170ml/6fl oz white wine
Salt and ground black pepper
½ handful fresh tarragon leaves, or 2 tablespoons freeze-dried tarragon
55-75ml/2-3fl oz single cream

There are many elaborate ways to cook a plain chicken breast, which butchers call a chicken suprême when it includes the first joint of the wing – it provides the stubby bit sticking out of that 1950s-60s bistro triumph, chicken Kiev. During the 1970s-80s, a chicken suprême was frequently the pièce de resistance of a nouvelle cuisine menu, to be used in a disastrous dish like Chicken Breast Stuffed with Mango in a Coulis of Malibu. (At the kitchens of Bibendum in those days, the noble purists Simon Hopkinson and Henry Harris compiled an atrocious list of real examples they'd heard of.) But I absolve the piece of poultry of mockery. Chicken breast is lean, inexpensive, and quick to do. It can be easily embellished even by unimaginative cooks, and when it is given a rich sauce, any limitations of taste due to the chicken's poor upbringing won't be seriously called into question.

Which brings us to Chicken Tarragon – an excellent choice to accompany something stolid like potato kugel (page 86). Its third ingredient, cream, I infrequently use because regular reliance is not very healthy, and cream sauces in my opinion usually taste poncy and dinnerpartyish. Certainly there are ways to make sauces velvety using less animal fat, such as the substitution Michel Guérard popularised, fromage blanc. But cream is perfect with tarragon and chicken, and a fromage blanc alternative takes second place. There isn't that much cream in this recipe.

Flatten out the chicken suprêmes with the heel of your hand. To a hot sauté pan, first add the oil, then add the butter so it doesn't burn. Brown both sides of the suprêmes, then stir in the wine and tarragon. Cook the chicken over moderate heat, adding some seasoning and a bit of water if necessary when the alcohol has boiled off.

After about 15 minutes, remove the chicken and reduce the liquid if necessary. About 30 seconds before the finish, add cream and correct the seasoning. For this dish the sauce should be poured over the chicken on each plate.

POULE AU POT AÏOLI

1 large chicken or capon
1 large onion, skinned and
    halved
3 leeks, washed, trimmed and
    split lengthwise
2 carrots, trimmed and split into
    lengthwise quarters
1 handful parsley, chopped
Fresh tarragon (if available)
1 celery heart with leaves,
    quartered
1 bay leaf
750g/27oz small or medium
    boiling potatoes, scrubbed
2-3 carrots, trimmed and thinly
    sliced into circles
About 20 whole black or green
    peppercorns
Salt and ground black pepper

For the aïoli:
2 eggs
Salt and a dash of cayenne
225ml/8fl oz unfancy olive and
    vegetable oils, mixed
1 tablespoon lemon juice
4 large garlic cloves, finely
    chopped, or 3 tablespoons
    garlic purée
½ handful parsley, finely
    chopped

This can be a fairly quick big family meal. It takes not much more than an hour. Put it on and leave.

For stage I, if the chicken isn't absolutely freshly killed, wash it inside and out and rinse the cavity with some lemon juice. Put it in a pot only a bit bigger than it is. Fill with water and add all the ingredients down to, but not including, the potatoes. Bring to the boil quickly, then immediately reduce the heat, cover the pot and simmer for an hour.

Stage II consists of making the aïoli, a garlicky mayonnaise. Use a blender or food processor and blend together the whole eggs and salt, then slowly dribble in the oils until the mixture thickens. Add the lemon juice, garlic, parsley and seasoning.

For stage III, add the potatoes, circular carrots and peppercorns to the poaching pot and simmer for about 20 minutes more until the potatoes are just soft.

When done, remove the chicken and carve some slices and chunks onto four plates, accompanied by leeks, potatoes and circular carrots – ignore the onion, celery and long carrots that joined the pot in stage I as most of their flavour will have been lost to the liquid. Add to each serving about 3 tablespoons of the strained stock (with aïoli it's unnecessary to thicken it with a roux or cream), then a large dollop of the aïoli should go right on the side of each plate.

Fish

KEDGEREE 1 AND KEDGEREE 2

Kedgeree 1:
250g/9oz butter
¼ teaspoon curry powder
200g/7oz tinned tuna in oil
4-6 eggs, hardboiled with whites chopped and yolks crumbled
280g/10oz dry weight brown rice, cooked
Salt and ground black pepper
2 tablespoons lemon juice
Cayenne pepper

Kedgeree 2:
800g-1kg/30oz-2¼lb Finnan Haddie (strongly recommended), or ordinary smoked haddock
1 bay leaf
110g/4oz butter
1 onion, chopped
280g/10oz uncooked basmati rice (makes about 1 litre/36oz cooked)
4 eggs, hardboiled
1 teaspoon ground cumin
½ teaspoon turmeric
Small knob of butter
200g/7oz cooked shrimps (optional)
Fresh coriander, chopped
Single cream to taste

Though it basically consists of rice, flaked fish and hardboiled eggs, kedgeree is many things to many men – including my father Freddie, who used to make what I've called Kedgeree 1 for Sunday night tea. I don't know if my boast that Freddie's kedgeree was utterly inauthentic should impress anyone, since I have read that the authentic Indian dish has onions and lentils and lacks fish. My family loved it anyway.

Kedgeree 2 displays the completely opposite kind of inauthenticity. It is a poem of skilfully interwoven special flavours that start with Finnan Haddie, the haddock smoked on the bone over a peat-reek. Kedgeree 2 would suit a bunch of hoorays after topping a fox, Kedgeree 1 the engineroom crew of a minesweeper (where I think Freddie first mastered his dish).

Kedgeree 1. Melt the butter in a pan and reserve. Use the remains of butter in the pan to sauté the hint of curry powder. Turn off heat, add the tuna and mix it with all the melted butter, the rice and egg whites. Add salt, pepper and the lemon juice and heat it through if desired. Pile on plates and garnish with crumbled egg yolks and sprinkles of cayenne.

Kedgeree 2. Cover the fish with cold water, add bay leaf, bring to the boil and turn off heat – the fish will be cooked. Drain the fish, *reserving the stock*. Melt the butter and sauté the onion until soft, then add rice, stirring together the onion and the dry rice in the pan. Turn up the heat, slowly add all the fish stock and fresh water as necessary (not too much) until the rice is cooked with some slight chewiness.

Meanwhile, skin, bone and flake the fish; shell the eggs and chop them roughly. Sauté the cumin and turmeric in the small knob of butter in a large pan. Drain the rice. Lightly stir the rice, eggs and fish, and the shrimp if using, into the pan. Add the coriander and enough cream to make the whole dish moist. This dish is best if left for a bit and reheated. Before serving, mix in some more single cream.

HERRING WITH POTATO SALAD

1kg/2¼lb waxy, not floury,
  potatoes, halved or quartered
  if large
2-3 tablespoons of *one* of the
  following alternatives:
  Capers, chopped if large
  Spring onions, finely chopped
  Red onion, finely sliced
  Carrot, cut in very fine disc
  slices
  Gherkins or cornichons,
  chopped
  ½ handful parsley, chopped

For the vinaigrette:
170ml/6fl oz plain vegetable oil,
  such as groundnut or
  sunflower
2 tablespoons prepared
  mayonnaise
4-5 garlic cloves, finely chopped
1 teaspoon dry mustard, or 1
  tablespoon prepared Dijon
  mustard
1 teaspoon sugar
1 squirt liquid Maggi
55ml/2fl oz white wine vinegar,
  malt vinegar, or lemon juice
Salt and ground black pepper

A Swedish country hotel smorgasbord will have ten or fifteen kinds of pickled herring in little dishes on the buffet table, each marinated in a subtly different combination of sweet, sour and herbal flavours; nearby, there are typically awesome pickling jars that display more herrings with beautiful sliced vegetables in liquid. My two favourites are Bismarck herring, whole flat fillets done in a sour marinade with rings of raw white onion, and a nameless variety with a sweetish dill marinade that I buy by the tub. The alternative agreeable ways of eating most forms of pickled herring are on a large plain white plate with a dollop of soured cream plus a large, whole peeled boiled potato, or else just with a warm potato salad. So here is a good recipe for the latter.

Boil the potatoes in their skins until they are just tender. Drain. When they have cooled slightly, peel them and roughly slice further if necessary so all pieces are about the size of chequers or a little larger. Add to the potatoes one of the listed alternatives.

The strongly flavoured vinaigrette should be made in a food processor (the prepared mayonnaise is a great help to emulsify the oil and keep it mixed with the other ingredients, and to coat the potatoes), and applied as soon as possible while the potatoes are still fairly hot. When ready to serve, add more vinaigrette – some will have soaked in – and the parsley, and correct the seasoning. This potato salad is best served warm.

QUEEN SCALLOPS ON THE HALF SHELL

16-24 queen scallops
4 rashers sweet cure streaky
    bacon
Butter, chilled
Flat-leaf parsley
Coarse salt
Garlic purée, or finely chopped
    garlic

Queen scallops are smaller and can work out cheaper than big scallops. They are actually a different species, but they look and taste not unlike big scallops – that is, they have one of the richest shellfish flavours. According to Jane Grigson, the best fish restaurant in Cherbourg just put them under a very hot grill until they opened. Then they were turned over, given about three more minutes, and brought to the table like that to be eaten with bread and butter. At the other extreme, chef Rick Stein once published a fanatical recipe involving juliennes of inserted vegetables that were cooked to different timings in Vouvray and butter, and then the shells were resealed with puff pastry. My baked scallops are between the two as far as troublesomeness goes – closer to Cherbourg – and depend on a familiarly favourable combination of tastes with bacon and garlic. They make a perfect starter for a private party of my guests such as The Cranium Club, The Ladies Who Lunch, or a football team's testimonial dinner.

This is dead easy if you approach the situation like the Ford assembly line, using scissors, a small sharp knife, tweezers and a table knife as your tools. If your fishmonger, like mine, supplies fresh queens ready-opened on the half shell, fine – the service can be worth a little extra cost. Otherwise, put them all one layer deep in a baking pan, the flatter side of the shells facing up, and give them a blast very close under the grill, or a few minutes in a very hot oven, until they open. Then pull off the flat shells.

Meanwhile, panfry the bacon rashers until nearly crisp, then cut them crosswise into a fine julienne. Dice some cold butter exactly the size of real dice. Cut off a few dozen leaves of the parsley; and lay out a few pinches of coarse salt on a surface.

Using your tweezers, give each scallop an equal fraction of bacon slivers, one cube of butter, two leaves of parsley and about three crystals of salt. Finally, using the point of a table knife, smear a 1cm/½in long tubular squeeze of garlic purée, or the equivalent of finely chopped garlic, on to each scallop.

Just before serving, pop the scallops back into a very hot oven for about 6 minutes or directly under a grill for about 3 minutes. Toast soldiers make good accompaniments, or baked puff pastry crescents if you want to be fancy. A small fork and a teaspoon are the best utensils.

PASTA WITH SMOKED SALMON

55-110g/2-4oz smoked salmon,
    chopped
500g/18oz fresh tagliatelle
45g/1½oz butter
3 tablespoons single cream
½ handful parsley, chopped
Salt and cayenne pepper

When my friend Beth Coventry cooked at Green's in SW1 next door to my old pub The Unicorn, she often gave me little parcels of smoked salmon trimmings that were too bitty for Green's fancy customers. The following was a nice way for The Unicorn's plainer customers to polish them off.

If the smoked salmon is at all dry, first let the chopped bits refresh in some lemon juice for an hour.

Cook the tagliatelle in plenty of boiling water until al dente, then drain and put into the serving bowl. Stir in the butter, cream, parsley, smoked salmon, salt, and finally just enough cayenne pepper for the eater to get the point.

MOULES SOHO

1kg/2¼lb healthy mussels from Wales, or somewhere else vouchworthy
110g/4oz butter
200g/7oz shallots, chopped
1 handful parsley, chopped
250-400ml/9-14fl oz fish stock, dry white wine, or a combination (optionally with saffron added)
Sprinkle of chilli seeds, as garnish

Oysters were a poor man's dish in Dickensian times, or so legend has it. Nowadays a £2 bag of mussels prepared this way – a bit soupier than moules marinière – will feed four, for either a starter or a main course, and I'd be hard put to say the moules aren't as enjoyable as oysters. As has already been said, very good quick fish stock can be made from dried Ikan Bilis granules, sold at oriental groceries in little jars.

Soak or brush the mussels in running water, pulling off some of the stragglier beards and discarding floaters: note that cleaning off mud is desirable, pulling off beards is optional (mussel beards are organic and don't affect their taste), but discarding dead mussels is compulsory.

Put the butter and shallots in a deep pot and swizzle over heat for five minutes, then add the parsley and the fish stock and/or white wine. Bring to the boil, then add the mussels. Cover the pan and steam with the lid on, shaking the pan vigorously once or twice to toss them around until all the mussels are opened in 6 or 7 minutes (any that haven't opened after that should be considered DOA, and discarded). Serve in large bowls garnished with chilli seeds and with chunks of bread.

STEAMED TROUT

4 whole cleaned trout the right
    size for one person, heads
    left on
200g/7oz butter
Handful fresh tarragon
Ground black pepper
3 tablespoons lemon juice
Salt
280g/10oz brown rice

This is actually microwaved trout. Steaming fish is one of the limited number of things a microwave oven can do perfectly. We tried to think of a menu name that frankly hinted at the process without putting off people who are prejudiced against electronic cooking. The best we could come up with was Waved Trout. On reflection that sounded like something from the hairdresser. So the blackboard euphemistically refers to this dish as steamed trout, and we call it microwaved trout in the kitchen.

Ideally, a steamed fish is a cleaned whole fish with its head intact. To achieve this on a stove top, you would use, if you owned one, a long salmon kettle with a fitted perforated steaming tray and lid. They cost a fortune and take up a lot of cupboard space. Since you can only put non-metallic things in a microwave, the ideal container for steaming the fish in there is a long plastic box with loose lid that fits inside diagonally. Otherwise, a long casserole with lid works. A lidless container can be attempted, but you must at least wrap the fish in paper, because while cooking, bits of it will pop and spatter.

Below I've suggested brown rice with it because it makes a simple yet delightful accompaniment. Slightly more ambitious is a rice pilaff with peas: soften some chopped onion in fat in a pan, add uncooked basmati or long grain rice, stir in some fish stock and cook until the rice is tender; finally add seasoning, butter, and some delicate cooked peas.

Rinse the trout and pat them dry inside and out with a clean tea towel. Mash together the butter, tarragon leaves, ground pepper and lemon juice. Spread the mixture inside the trout putting a little down their gullets, too, then sprinkle them with salt and give them a few minutes' rest.

Cook the rice according to packet instructions, then keep it warm in a pot with the lid on. From here on, directions depend on the power, size and wave-scattering capabilities of your own microwave. The microwave's instruction book may resourcefully guide you about the length of time steamed fish should get. If you're on your own, cook two fish at a time, give them about 4 minutes, and watch through the window. (See above about the need for a lid, or at least a paper wrapping.) Don't overcook the fish. It's better to take them out too soon, check for doneness and put them back for a little longer if necessary.

Opposite:
Salt Cod Aïoli with potatoes,
page 97

≈≈≈

SALT COD AÏOLI

1kg/2¼lb salt cod
1kg/2¼lb waxy yellow potatoes,
    boiled, peeled and sliced
1 onion, halved
1 bay leaf
Aïoli (see page 90 for the
    method, but for this version
    all the oil used should be
    finest extra virgin olive, and
    finely chop a whole head of
    garlic into it because it must
    be very strong)
110-150g/4-6oz good black
    olives, stoned and halved
2 lemons, quartered

We are in classic French provincial country with this one: see *Larousse Gastronomique*, Elizabeth David, Simon Hopkinson; or don't – stay put. My version isn't a virtuoso purée of salt cod, oil and milk, just a simple plate of the flaked fish with potatoes and an exceptional form of garlicky mayonnaise. Continental grocers sell salt cod and to this day it's especially likely to be available just before Lent. The brandade, or puréed, rendition from around Nîmes was a penitential dish for Good Friday. After fame beckoned, the postwar French housewife would struggle to combine different ingredients from three pans on the go (described in daunting detail by La David). Later came the food processor, and for a while the components went into that. I rather prefer the main ingredients unmushed, as follows:

Soak the salt cod in cold water for hours, then rinse out all the salt you can (plenty will remain no matter what) in slowly running cold water overnight. A full 24 hour soak and rinse is best.

Boil, peel and slice the potatoes and prepare the aïoli. Cut the fish in pieces and about 20 minutes before eating, poach for about 10 minutes in water with only the onion and bay leaf added. Drain, remove bones and skin, and flake.

Serve little piles of flaked fish on big plates with the potatoes and aïoli, garnished with halved black olives and quartered lemons (picture it!). A central bowl of crisp raw cauliflower florets would be an ideal aïoli companion vegetable, and penitentially white, too.

Left:
The Billy Wilder Special with
sausages, page 108

EEL PIE

675g/1½lb eel, head off, cut into 4cm/1½in sections by the fishmonger (eels are available live from a tank in the Chinese fish shop in Newport Place, Soho, but don't watch as they execute one for you)
30g/1oz butter
2 tablespoons flour
3 eggs, whisked
Salt and ground black pepper
1 packet frozen puff pastry

For the court bouillon:
1 litre/1¾ pints water
½ handful parsley, finely chopped
170ml/6fl oz malt vinegar
10 black peppercorns
½ carrot, thinly sliced
½ lemon, plus its juice squeezed into the bouillon
1 bay leaf

In 1995 the Museum of London published a lovely book of photographs and historical notes about the rise and slow decline of the London eel and pie shop. It brought home to me that eels with their distinctive flavour and their usual retail provenance remained a greater force to contend with than the Earlham Street market stall snacks I knew:

> Inside, a typical shop was fitted out with marble tables, wooden benches, white tiled walls and huge mirrors. Sawdust was sprinkled on the floor so that customers could spit out the eel bones. In the kitchens there would be large ovens, where the pies were cooked, and large water racks to preserve the eels. Opening hours were normally from ten in the morning to twelve at night. Everything was kept fastidiously clean, and the shops thus retained their own grandeur.[9]

There's a lot to be said about the social significance and simple design splendour of eel and pie shops, but if I go on I'd only be cribbing from the book which you should read if the subject interests you. The thing that mainly concerns us are eel pies. Apparently they are no more – at least not in the eel and pie shops.

Sometime in the not too distant past, the brain-damaged muse of history caused East End piemakers to phase out eel pies. The Museum of London book doesn't satisfactorily explain why.[10] What eel and pie shops now uniformly feature are (1) eels, either stewed or jellied, (2) meat pies, (3) mashed potatoes, and (4) 'liquor' – a soupy parsley sauce with chillis and vinegar. But no *eel* pies. The divorce between the eel and pastry seems to have become final.

---

9 From the historical essay by Paolo Hewitt in *Eels, Pie and Mash*, by Chris Clunn and others. London 1995.
10 My guess is that people are iffy about contending with fish bones concealed under a pastry crust. They preferred eating visible slices of bony eel in a bowl to eating bony eel concealed within a pie, so stewed and jellied eels in bowls became predominant and eel pie shops became extinct. But that's sheer conjecture. By the way, the recipe given doesn't solve this problem – the bones have to be spat out.

Until now. My gross reinvention was necessary since there seem no current models to adapt. Calling it pseud would be accurate – I don't think the original would have had eggs whipped in to produce a sort of rich vinegary custard. But Australians love pies, as even the eel and pie shop proprietors admit, so I'm the right sort of foreigner for the job. We might not be shoring up the monarchy, but we are certainly prepared to lead the eel pie restoration.

I've tried using less vinegar, and cream instead of egg. This lemony, eggy version seems best. The cooked egg will precipitate in tiny flecks in the eel sauce, but because it's so gelatinous it isn't like mayonnaise 'curdle' and it doesn't affect flavour or texture. In common with steak and kidney and most other meat pies, this has a top crust only. It's possible to make a complete pie using waterproof shortcrust pastry. If one made a complete eel pie and floated it in more parsley liquor – fish stock and parsley with a butter and flour roux – like Pie and Pea Floater (page 36), the combination could be called Eel Pie Island. And that, coincidentally, is the name of a famous old jazz venue in the Thames near Richmond.

You need a medium pie dish or casserole for this. Simmer the eel in the court bouillon for about 20 minutes, removing it when tender. At this stage you can easily remove the spines and most of the bones, which I advise (or if you are fanatical, you may try to remove them all). Remove the half lemon and bay leaf from the stock and discard.

Make a roux by melting the butter and stirring in the flour, then – to thicken – adding the eel stock very gradually at first while stirring. Off the heat, add the whisked eggs and the eel pieces and correct the seasoning. Put in more chopped parsley if the taste and appearance suggest it.

Put in the pie dish or casserole. Roll out some pastry and make a 0.3cm/⅛in thick lid, crimping round the edges. Bake for 20 minutes at 200°C/400°F/Gas 6. Serve with mashed potatoes (page 62). Warn diners 'plenty of bones – they're part of the dish', and provide side dishes for them.

COLEY JUMBO

Coley fish, boned and flaked
Court bouillon of Ikan Bilis
    granules (dried fish stock),
    sliced onion, coriander and
    peppercorns
Onions, roughly chopped
Olive oil
Tomato purée
Fresh hot chilli peppers, finely
    chopped
Garlic, finely chopped
Tinned tomato
Malt vinegar
Fresh coriander, slightly chopped
Salt and ground black pepper

Pub drinkers are well disposed towards spiced-up, pungent food tastes, especially because beer and spirits rather than wine are the usual accompaniments. I daresay this dish could be successful either with a Real Ale man at the local or a Gibson-wielding publisher at the Groucho. It tastes great as a cold canapé on thick slices of granary bread or ciabatta, or as a warm main dish alongside basmati rice. One of the objects of grande cuisine is to intensify flavours by reducing and thickening, but sometimes it's nice to achieve full flavour and just let the dish stay runny, as with this. Its name is my pun on gumbo.

Coley, by the way, is in the cod family, and there are many common names for it – sometimes saithe, and in the USA, pollock. It is occasionally derided as cat food, but that's because it is fresh, strong-textured and one of the cheaper fishes in the market. The substitution of cod would make a more expensive but not necessarily finer version. I haven't given exact quantities because it is best to feel your own way experimentally with this dish according to taste, the anticipated number to feed, and the availability of ingredients.

Poach the fish for about a minute in the court bouillon and reserve in the liquid. Sauté the onions in olive oil until almost soft. Add tomato purée and chilli and sauté thoroughly to fully release their flavours. Add the garlic, the tinned tomato including liquid, a small amount of vinegar and plentiful coriander. Simmer a bit, then turn off the heat and add the fish with some fish stock and correct the seasoning. The consistency should be a quite thick lumpy soup. Let the mixture rest for about half an hour before chilling or reheating to serve cold or hot. Serve with a little chopped coriander as garnish.

Charcoal grilled

When I recently redid my domestic kitchen I had a commercial charcoal grill built alongside my cooker under a powerful new extract hood. 'Charcoal' grills made for caterers usually have – as mine does – multiple gas jets under ceramic stones under a cast-steel grating. The ceramic heats up nearly red hot but isn't consumed. So the charcoal is not contributed by fuel such as mesquite or oak chips, it's what the food starts to turn into. If you can accept the limitation of receiving no contributory taste it's a great way to cook at home as well as in a pub, and I'm sure it will become the home cooking method of the future.

But some cautionary notes. While chargrilling is a good low-fat way to cook because fat isn't usually added and any fat already in tends to become consumed, not everything you might think of is suitable. Fatty steaks or chops produce excessive smoke and leave a nasty burned fat residue on the cooked meat, so meat like that should first be scrupulously trimmed to remove as much fat as possible. For a similar reason, hamburgers are better pan-fried and fat drained, and forget about 'barbecued' spare ribs – they would quickly burn to carbon. They should be roasted (page 74). Squid and fish steaks are great done on a grill, but with them, fat needs to be *added*: the grill's steel grating should be painted with some vegetable oil just before slapping on the fish, or they will stick like a superglue accident. Stylistically, serious grillmasters and grillmistresses produce a diamond design that is generated by the grill first carbonising parallel lines in one direction, then a second set with the meat or fish turned about 90 degrees.

I won't say much more, except that at the East Coast Grill in Cambridge, Massachusetts, where grilling has become an art, I've observed that their general approach is to roll or rub the meat or fish with something, then grill it, then baste it with something.

Pending ceramic grill prices coming down to domestic levels, you could cook the following on an outdoors barbecue using real charcoal and the highest possible heat you can achieve. A domestic overhead grill produces much less heat and no real fat consumption, though you could try it. Panfrying might be a better alternative. For gastronomic charcoal grilling, the reference I recommend is The East Coast Grill's cookbook, *The Thrill of the Grill*.[11]

LAMB CHOPS, LAMB CUTLETS

Take note of the previous comments (page 101) on the need to trim fat assiduously before chargrilling. Lamb cutlets are on the borderline, chargrillwise, because the remaining fat will probably still burn and their thin rib bones are pretty sure to carbonise. Lamb chops are a bit thicker and meatier, so they chargrill rather better. If you buy garlic in purée form, which I recommend for recipes like this, make a paste of it and some chopped rosemary and smear it on both sides of the cutlets or chops before grilling.

STEAK WITH CORIANDER CRUST AND FRITES

4 entrecôte steaks at least
    1.5cm/½in thick
1 tablespoon balsamic vinegar
1 tablespoon light vegetable oil
    (not olive)
1 tablespoon coriander seeds
55g/2oz matzo meal
Salt

For the frites:
2 litres/3½ pints groundnut, corn,
    or other vegetable oil
1kg/2¼lb good frying potatoes,
    such as Maris Piper or Desirée
2 large garlic cloves, unpeeled,
    the points snipped off
Coarse salt and fine salt

For many, a plainly grilled steak with pommes frites makes a perfect meal that could be eaten daily, so I won't say plain steak is boring, but the easy marinade and coating that follows turns it into something more special. It also precludes any need for mustard or ketchup, though of course some are compelled to add condiments whatever a steak's preparation. After experimentation, my pub features steak both with and without crust: 'steak plainly grilled' at a locally competitive price, and 'steak with coriander crust' for 50p more. (This crust is also delicious on a boned leg of lamb, making a nice change from the classic roast with garlic and rosemary.)

If you can't chargrill, the second best way to cook this is by pan grilling. I prefer those cast-iron grill pans or griddles made with corrugated bottoms because they allow a steak to both sear and sweat. The fat dripping out isn't trapped between steak and pan, and turned two ways the corrugations of the pan can make a diamond pattern. Either chargilling or pan grilling, to help blackening, I always put a little olive oil on a steak to be plainly grilled

---

11 By Chris Schlesinger & John Willoughby, New York, 1990.

as the French do, but the non-olive oil listed below for the coriander crusted steak works better with its other tastes. As for doneness, if I'm not told otherwise the customer gets it red in the middle and nearly black outside, which is easy on an almost red hot griddle provided the steak isn't so thin it cooks through before the outside blackens.

Trim any excess fat from the steaks. Marinate them for at least an hour in the vinegar and oil in order to get the rich tarry balsam flavour into the meat fibres.

Brown, but don't blacken, the coriander seeds without oil in a hot frying pan, then either crush them in a mortar and pestle, or mill them in a clean coffee grinder. (The coffee grinder blade is ideal for spices. To clean it afterwards, mince a slice of bread and wipe it out dry.) Mix the crushed or milled coriander with the matzo meal and salt.

When ready to serve, slap the dry mixture onto the meat and press it with the heel of your hand to make it stick, which it will. Flame-grill the steaks on iron bars or in an extremely hot griddle pan.

To explain about pommes frites that go with steak, I can do no better than quote (below) my dear friend Stephenie Bergman, a wonderful cook who lives in the south of France.

Stephenie's instructions, with my own interjections in square brackets:

'Heat the oil in a deep fryer [suggestion: to 150°C/300°F]. Peel and wash potatoes and cut them into big cubes. Put them in the chip basket with the garlic cloves, unpeeled, but with the points snipped off, and let the basket drop into the hot oil. Impossible to be exact about anything, but basically the oil is hot when you immerse the potatoes and then you lower the heat so the potatoes cook about 6 to 8 minutes. Take the basket out and turn off the heat at least for 30 minutes. [At serving time] reheat the oil and when it is very hot [suggestion: to about 185°C/360°F] immerse the chip basket once more until the chips look done. Drain. Put them on absorbent paper. Sprinkle with *gros sel* [coarse salt] and *petit sel* [fine salt], a tip from the very famous French chef Joël Robuchon, as you get both the crunchiness and the taste of the salt to contrast with the smooth inside of the chips. Certainly not to eat with fish – more like an entrecôte steak, or any grilled meat.'

GRILLED POUSSIN AND LEEKS

2 poussins, split as above
1 litre/1¾ pints homemade
    chicken stock, or water with
    one chicken cube

For the pre-grilling rub:
2 tablespoons garlic purée
2 tablespoons fresh rosemary, or
    2 teaspoons dried rosemary
4 tablespoons unfancy olive oil
Salt and ground black pepper

For the leeks:
3 leeks, white part only, washed
    and halved lengthwise
3 tablespoons extra virgin olive
    oil
2 tablespoons balsamic vinegar
Salt and ground black pepper

Grilling is the simplest way to cook young chickens that weigh 250-300g/9-11oz. They aren't so thick they are likely to blacken on the outside before becoming cooked within, nor is the meat susceptible to toughening on a grill like that of wood pigeon. To prepare, either 'butterfly' them (cut breast sides only down the middle) or split them in two; either way, flatten them with the heel of the hand. The excellent recipe below is adapted from Schlesinger and Willoughby.

Poach the poussins in the simmering chicken stock for a few minutes. (This isn't to sidestep toughness, but to lessen food-poisoning danger from any remaining rawness, as one ought to do nowadays. The recommendation was my GMTV 'superhint'.) Then remove and drain, reserving the stock for something else. Rub the poussins inside and out with garlic, rosemary, olive oil and seasoning, finally reflattening them with the heel of your hand. Put them on the hot grill skin-side down for about 15 minutes, and when the skin is brown and crispy, turn over and grill for 10 minutes.

The leeks go on the grill raw and plain near the end, starting with the cut side down, then turned after 3 or 4 minutes. When done, put the leeks in a bowl and toss with the oil, vinegar and seasoning. Garnish each poussin with a curly bunch of leeks to serve.

4 A SNACK WITH THE GARGLE

The Saloon Bar at the Prince Alfred

This chapter starts with egg dishes and sandwiches, often thought of as 'snacks' though they may be substantial meals, then goes on to ideas about nice accompaniments for serving casually with drinks. And as with almost all the recipes in this book, they either have their origin in pubs, or they are so reasonably laid-back that they could easily turn up there.

Food with drinks sounds an easy proposition but it's riddled with pitfalls. If anyone in Britain nowadays asked people to cocktail parties, the problem might resolve itself with 'cocktail snacks'. Remember them? Cream cheese and pickle rolled up in chilled white bread; bacon twisted round smoked oysters in prunes. Even if I was any help in that department, cocktail snacks seem fatuous and banal. They've really been over since the 1950s.

For the opposite extreme, the current interplay of food and fashion, I'm not much help either. You might check out *Vogue Entertaining*. I make fun of Condé Nast's bi-monthly Australian homemaking magazine, but I'm a loyal reader. Amid its catering for local seafood and produce, Eurochef adaptations, Cal-Ital imports and Thai concepts, its Recipe Index has a regular section devoted to 'food with drinks' featuring a range of complex snacks to be whipped, baked and skewered.

What I aspire to is neither. Maybe my idea of a snack with the gargle is what I think I would get if Stephane Audran said I should drop in to her place near Fontainebleau, or was that near Toulouse, on a Sunday afternoon (I'm fantasising). As I'm enjoying a few laughs with Philippe Noiret, I'd be downing a fabulous glass of country Burgundy, and – of this I'm positive – reaching for a bready slab of anchoïade or pissaladière (page 122). Just down from heaven, François Truffaut strolls over and I include him in the conversation. Did I mention that I'm divinely fluent in French?

Eggs

In a pub, omelettes are the cook's nightmare because they require 90 per cent of one's attention for a specific seven or eight minutes. Every customer wants them at some stage if he/she's not feeling well, wants a light lunch, or is dieting. I was taken to lunch at the Étoile in the early '70s when it was a home of restaurant tradition. At the time I was working in a night club, so it was very early for me and all I wanted was an omelette which wasn't on the menu. The maître d'hotel (Monty?) embarrassingly announced to all the customers in the small dining room, 'Ah, madame hasn't had her breakfast!'

At my pub, I do omelettes and other forms of cooked-to-order eggs cheerfully, provided we're not too busy. The most-requested pub omelette is probably a cheese (mild Cheddar) omelette with chips. I try to serve them with salads, rather than potatoes cooked in more fat. The following recipes include two egg dishes which need cooking to order, and two you can prepare several hours or a whole day before.

FRIED EGGS AND BLACK PUDDING WITH HASH BROWNED POTATOES

This is a great hit when I have time to make it. I needn't provide elaborate detail. Eggs for frying have to be very fresh or the yolks will annoyingly break. Sizzle them in butter on a griddle, medium to high heat, basting the yolks with some of the molten butter before the pan gets too hot and the butter darkens. Black pudding, a great favourite from the north of England (it's a sausage made from blood, of course), can be plopped on the griddle after the eggs for a couple of minutes, or a few slices can just be microwaved for a minute under some kitchen paper – it's a perfectly decent way to bring up the taste since the pudding has enough added fat to cook itself.

Hash browns are a Yankee wrinkle on sautéed potatoes. Use

uncooked waxy rather than mealy potatoes, such as Ulster Sceptre, Pentland Javelin or Belle de Fontenay, and chop them into large dice, either peeled, or just scrubbed but unpeeled – the latter is fine. No parboiling. Melt plenty of butter, beef dripping or lard in a heavy sauté pan and press the potatoes down into a cake, turning not very often to allow some crusts to build. When halfway done, take the pan off the heat and cover it with a lid or plate for a few minutes. (This is a vital step that gets the potatoes to *steam*.) Remove lid again, add salt, pepper, more fat if necessary dribbling down, and return to the heat for the final crusting.

THE BILLY WILDER SPECIAL (MATZO FRY WITH SAUSAGE)

Reading Maurice Zolotow's *Billy Wilder in Hollywood* a few years ago about one of my favourite film directors, I came across the following on a dish my husband also highly rates:

WALTER NEWMAN: ...One morning, as we started working... [Billy] said he had a marvelous *matzo brei* for his breakfast. I asked him politely, 'What is *matzo brei*?' Well, I thought he would jump out of his skin. He went beserk. He shouted, 'What, you, a Jewish boy from New York, Walter, you never ate *matzo brei*? But this is impossible.' I told him that furthermore I had never even heard of *matzo brei* until this moment. He could not get over it. He kept muttering for weeks things like, what could he expect from a schmuck who had never heard of *matzo brei*? Once he zeroes into something like *matzo brei*, he never lets go.

VICTORIA WILDER SETTEMBER [Billy's daughter]: I used to make *matzo brei* for daddy's breakfast. He said I made the best *matzo brei*, as good as his grandmother made. The idea is to break up the matzo but not crumble it. Then you have to soak it in warm milk five minutes. You should not soak it too long. And use plenty of butter. And three eggs. Stir up the matzo with the eggs before pouring into pan. I made it soft rather than as a pancake.[12]

Matzo brei, or matzo fry, originally a Passover dish, became a favourite of many European Jews. It has a comforting quality typical of many great eggy and starchy dishes. As Billy Wilder's indignation shows, to eat it is to love it. I decided that giving the dish a name my London media customers would rate wouldn't shamefully downplay the Diaspora. Served with an unkosher sausage (another Wilder breakfast preference) or black pudding, it's become extremely popular. You can't say English pubgoers are totally stick-in-the-mud about food, can you? We use my husband's version, which serves one:

Butter
1 regular-sized square of matzo (or 4 biscuit-sized), crushed in the hand but not pulverised
3 eggs, beaten as for an omelette or scramble
1 teaspoon chopped parsley
Salt and ground black pepper

Heat the butter in an omelette pan until it begins to sizzle. When absolutely ready to begin cooking, dash cold water into the bowl holding the crushed matzo, and after 20 seconds pour all the water off. Then add the eggs, parsley and seasoning to the matzo. Stir around and pour it all into the pan. Lift and scrape the egg and matzo from the bottom of the pan with a metal spoon until the fryup is still moist, but done. This method produces al dente matzos to my husband's taste. If you give the matzos a bit longer in the water they will be a bit more mushy, which some may prefer (five minutes in milk – Wilder's daughter's version – is ridiculous!). My quantities given above are for an individual portion because as with other omelettes, this dish is easiest to handle in batches made for one or two.

---

12 From Maurice Zolotow: *Billy Wilder in Hollywood*, London 1977.

CHOPPED EGG SALAD

3 onions, finely chopped
2 celery sticks, very finely chopped
75g/2½oz button mushrooms, thinly sliced or chopped
2 tablespoons vegetable oil
1 beef stock cube
8 eggs, hardboiled
100-150ml/4-6fl oz prepared mayonnaise
Salt and ground black pepper
Olives stoned and sliced, as garnish

Eggs seem to put Jewish cooks on their mettle, and like the Billy Wilder Special, chopped egg is another traditional favourite. My cousin by marriage Etah makes this superior version using mushroom as a secret ingredient, and I know it's renowned in parts of Dade and Broward counties in South Florida. There, it usually appears at lunch with other hors d'oeuvres such as chopped liver, Bismarck herring, potato salad and haimisha pickle, but my pub-goers find that it can handsomely stand on its own with a pint of beer. It's fine just on a plate with a piece of ciabatta bread, and a plump wodge of it with lettuce leaves inside a bread roll makes a soothing and completely satisfying sandwich filler.

Sauté the onions and celery in vegetable oil until onions are soft, then add mushrooms and continue cooking for a few minutes until they are just softened. Drain the oil and cool off the mixture in a bowl.

Mash the stock cube with the cold eggs and add to the vegetable mixture. Add enough mayonnaise gradually so the mixture is neither very dry nor very creamy. Correct the seasoning and garnish with sliced olives.

MAMABEL'S TORTILLA

1 large or 2 medium mild onions, thinly sliced
55ml/2fl oz unfancy olive oil
210-260g/7-9½oz potatoes, cooked and sliced
4 eggs, separated, yolks beaten, whites whisked to a peak, but not too dry
Lean chicken pieces, cooked, boned and diced (optional)
Semi-hot chillis (optional)
Small amount of broccoli, courgettes, aubergines, red peppers or peas, cooked (optional)
Salt and ground black pepper
75ml/2½fl oz unfancy olive oil

My former kitchen colleague Isabel Fernandez, a.k.a. Mamabel of Mohácar, España, taught me this. The basic ingredients are potato, onion and not all that many eggs. Tortillas often utilise leftovers, so by all means add bits of chicken, semi-hot chillis and other vegetables, but watch out that they aren't mushy, overvarious or overplentiful (in other words, avoid concocting the nondescript Technicolor Spanish Omelette of vulgar practice). It's delicious served hot; even better at room temperature. I cook these in a medium roundish-bottomed omelette pan and cut the tortillas into quarters.

Fry the onions in oil, then add the potatoes and cook until just barely golden. Add to beaten egg yolks plus any optional ingredients (not too many or too much of them). Season, then fold in the egg whites.

Heat the tortilla pan with plenty of olive oil and pour in the egg mixture. Keep the heat low to medium – what you are trying to achieve is at least three-quarters of the tortilla turned solid when the underside has become golden. At that well-judged point, cover the tortilla pan with a large plate and invert the tortilla onto the plate (plenty of oil makes this easy), then pour a few more good spoonfuls of oil in the pan, run it all round, and reinsert the tortilla undone side down. A few more well-judged minutes, and you then again invert it onto a plate. You should have a fluffy, oily, honeycombed cake. A green salad goes with it perfectly.

Sandwiches

FINE ROAST BEEF

The plain truth, slightly uncomfortable though it may be, is that a roast beef sandwich has been my most popular seller in Soho. But then there's lots of local competition for plain pub and Cal-Ital snacks, and a great sandwich is worth eating in preference to almost anything.

I always try to bump up sandwich flavour. My roast beef sandwich consists of two thick slices of ciabatta (olive oil) bread, which is soft, high and airy. The bottom slice is spread with commercial mayonnaise whipped up with garlic purée. It is covered with crisp Webb's lettuce leaves and tomato slices, then sprinkled with coarse ground black pepper done daily in the coffee grinder, then finely sliced pink beef, lots of it, an astounding event in Britain. The meat is salted. Then I spread prepared horseradish under the top slice of bread. It's cut in half, with two toothpicks to hold the sandwich together.

Opposite:
Focaccia toasts, Anchoïade and
Pissaladière, page 122; A Foggy
Day, page 138

BACON AND CABBAGE

Like so many happy discoveries, this was due to deficiency: there was nothing else in the house. The sandwich I then threw together turned out to be so satisfying that we weren't able to think of any improvement. I still use the ingredients I first came across through serendipity.

Steam half a head of separated cabbage leaves until soft, and allow to cool. It will provide enough cabbage for seconds. Panfry the bacon – I prefer a fairly sweet cure, like Canadian bacon, in streaky rather than back bacon form, and not paper-thin either. Toast some slices of granary bread, such as Vogel's, and spread one slice of toast for each sandwich with a combination of Dijon mustard and commercial mayonnaise. Fill each sandwich with about three thicknesses of cabbage leaf and two thicknesses of bacon.

CHOPPED EGG SALAD

See page 110 for preparing the egg salad. The canonical sandwich presentation is a thick wodge of chopped egg salad on two Webb's or Iceberg lettuce leaves on a fairly soft poppy-seeded Kaiser (crown-shaped) roll; but any roll, or even ciabatta bread, is excellent. Buttering the roll makes the sandwich noticeably more luxurious.

Left:
Noodle Bake with Roast
Vegetables, page 131

Side dishes

COB NUTS

Plates of nuts and crisps have always been freebies at bars in America and at hotel and cocktail bars, but not in English pubs where tradition invariably sides with meanness (we don't receive tips either). So a number of years ago I began to stand up for generosity during cob nut season.

Our cob nuts come from Kent and are eaten raw. Related to filberts and hazelnuts, they come beautifully wrapped by Mother Nature in an outer leafy carapace. Under that is a shell a bit too hard for the teeth, and within that, a rather superior nut.

During the season I have a couple of big bowls of cob nuts on the bar. A typical customer has to first be told what they are – lots of rich public relations is developed right there – and then grapple with opening a few. The right way is to strip off the carapace and crack the shells with a nutcracker. The wrong way is to go off with the nutcracker in your pocket.

After losing about ten nutcrackers at The Three Greyhounds, I decided to just leave a couple of large hammers on the bar. Either these lacked the appeal of nutcrackers or they were too heavy to steal. Their presence led to a lot of pounding, but on balance I thought it was good that our newly provided weathered-look pub tables and bar were slowly taking the real beating that their distressed finish aspired to.

PICKLED ONIONS

Pickled onions at least deserve notice because they are very English. Notice, but not attention. Their crude taste is thought to accompany cheese well, and so they are sometimes found on the side of the Ploughman's Lunch plate. Onions in malt vinegar with salt and coarse spices ('They bite back' is the motto of one preparation) isn't my idea of a gastronomic treat, so I avoid using them.

PICKLED EGGS

32 cloves
8 eggs, hardboiled and shelled
¾ teaspoon dry mustard
¾ teaspoon salt
Ground black pepper
450ml/16fl oz white wine vinegar
or distilled vinegar (not malt
vinegar)

Housewives in Pennsylvania used to save most of the juice from pickled beetroot to pickle hardboiled eggs, for eating as snacks with beer (relayed by James Beard). Commercial pickled eggs are unsubtly harsh-tasting, so I like the idea of pink eggs that are made with pickling juice used for the second time. Here is another delicate way to pickle eggs, adapted from Irma S Rombauer and Marion Rombauer Becker's indispensable book, *The Joy of Cooking*.

Stick four cloves into each egg at the quarter points around the egg's equator. Make a paste of the mustard, salt and pepper, using a little of the vinegar. Boil the rest of the vinegar and add the paste to it. Put the cloved eggs in a glass preserves jar and pour the boiling vinegar over them. Seal the jar and keep it in a cool place for two weeks. Pickled eggs are very good served sliced with cold cuts and salads, or as hors d'oeuvres with drinks.

BEETROOT

The Russians, the Dutch, the French and the Yanks like beets too, but of course the English give no quarter to foreign beet-lovers. Over here we call it beetroot, and eat it by the ton, pickled. Not bad. More than just beets hyped by a spin doctor. Here are a few simple things to do with beetroot if you see uncooked ones at the greengrocers.

Buy smallish beetroot for preference and wash them gently. Don't puncture their skins or the tasty juice will escape. Step one is always to simmer them in a little water until they are tender (squeeze gingerly to find out, don't puncture them with a fork) – this takes about 30 to 45 minutes. Then cool them in running water and peel off their skins.

As an optional step two, which makes a nice accompaniment for pork, the precooked sliced beetroot can be sautéed with butter, chopped spring onions, parsley and tarragon, with a little balsamic vinegar added at the end.

The pickling option is to deposit the sliced beetroot in a jar with sliced onions, peppercorns, whole allspice berries and a few whole cloves, then cover them with wine vinegar and stash them away for a few weeks. Put a plateful on the bar or the coffee table with a few toothpicks alongside the beer nuts, and they will disappear even more quickly.

COLESLAW

1 medium to large white
    cabbage, shredded
½ carrot, finely shredded
½ small onion, finely sliced
½ pickled beetroot, julienned
55g/2oz salty black olives, stoned
    and chopped, as garnish
    (optional)

For the dressing:
150ml/5fl oz olive oil (do use
    olive oil, though it doesn't
    have to be the greatest)
55ml/2fl oz commercial
    mayonnaise
3 tablespoons lemon juice
1 teaspoon caraway seeds
    (alternatively, celery seeds)
1 teaspoon salt, and ground
    black pepper

Coleslaw (which should be spelt as one word because it was originally *kohlslau*) is basically shredded cabbage in a sourish dressing. It's good with seafood salads or as a very reasonable accompaniment for a meat sandwich, either on the side or built in. In American fast food places, a sugary mayonnaise coleslaw is served alongside everything, usually in a fluted paper cup. English supermarkets sell expensively made-up sugary mayonnaisey versions too. Here's a nicer way to do it.

Shake up all the dressing ingredients in a jar, then toss with the shredded and chopped ingredients. Refrigerate. When ready to serve, toss the coleslaw and mix the dressing through again. Optionally, garnish with chopped black olives at the final stage.

PUB GARNISHES AND RELISHES

It's still possible to drop into urban caffs and find that the food, however noble in its simplicity, is mismatched against an elaborate collection of pickles, chutneys and relishes, not to mention an even more staggering array of bottled sauces and condiments. I used to associate big assortments of garnishes and condiments with hopeful attempts to mask the nature of dodgy food, partly because history bore me out. (The sweets and spices of Elizabethan cooking were brave attempts to hide the stink of unrefrigerated food going on the turn, largely successful as far as the appreciation of the rest of Europe was concerned.) But life has taught me that applied condiments have nothing to do with the quality or taste of the underlying food. People just like burying food in familiar flavours.

So I've stopped worrying that my sensitively fried cod in matzo meal usually gets ketchup dumped on it by both natives and tourists. If they love it that way, what do I care? It might even be true that ketchup eaters have a subtractive part of their brains next to their gastronomic neurones that completely eliminates the ketchup molecules, thus allowing them to have pure judgements about my fish. I like to think so.

Which is all to say that the several garnishes, relishes and condiments I keep as important adjuncts to pub food are there either because I think they are necessary myself, or because I'd get sick of explaining every time why there wasn't any. Here is my own small portfolio:

Branston Pickle For its provenance and ingredients, see page 126. Pubs aren't living up to their customers' expectations if they don't put spoonfuls of Branston on their bread and cheese (Ploughman's Lunch) plates.

Piccalilli In America the word means a sort of salmagundi of pickle made from green tomatoes, cucumber, green peppers, whatever, but for us in England it has come to mean only one thing: cauliflower pickle in a sweet-piquant yellow sauce. As such, piccalilli makes a reasonable alternative to Branston as a sidekick for bread and cheese. It's also useful for cold meats and pies as a more proletarian relish than Cumberland sauce.

Mango chutney The indisputable mother of chutneys; great

with curries. I keep it handy in the kitchen in case anyone asks, and otherwise sometimes use it instead of Branston or piccalilli.

Malt vinegar Usually asked for by customers who have ordered a dish that includes chips. I keep our cruet vinegar in a wine bottle, corked by one of those French tubular metal pourers. I also put whole chillis in the bottle.

Heinz tomato ketchup Now and forever, still the condiment champion; required by most of the other customers who don't ask for vinegar. The brand name on the bottle is taken to be its mark of authenticity, so I dispense the bottles as bought.

Mustard Funnily enough, not frequently asked for by customers. I use Dijon mustard in certain dishes and on certain sandwiches, but it generally has no public presence. For sausages, I keep available a little pan of English mustard made from dry mustard powder.

Tabasco, Worcestershire and Maggi sauces I keep these for professional use only, dispensing drinks and cooking.

Dips and spreads

People who want to serve drinks to guests first tend to think of dishing out wine and cheese, or if cocktails are planned, hors d'oeuvres and canapés. They are supposed to be sound nibbles that go well with drink. I beg to differ.

Cheese makes a lousy accompaniment for wine. A decent cheese will mask the taste of *any* wine. If you insist on having cheese as a snack with drinks, your drinks need to measure up. They'd better be spirits, or fortified wine such as port, Madeira or a rich sherry.

What about hors d'oeuvres and canapés? They *can* be wonderful. I've been to a party catered excellently with such by Celia Keyworth's Food. Lorna Wing Ltd does parties where the canapés are miniature hot dogs, hamburgers and wedges of cake. She's produced tiny fish and chips canapés wrapped in miniature *Financial Times* pages. She catered for my own wedding reception with a more normal canapé banquet in a sequence of courses, a delightful butler delivering bitesize mouthfuls off a silver tray. But for an informal gathering you don't need butler or silver tray, nor should you turn in desperation to slices of buttered white bread around asparagus, and stuffed prunes. I think the game's up socially if one ever finds oneself stuffing a prune.

What you really want is something more than a bowl of crisps, something less than a buffet lunch. Just a few delicious things on a table that your friends can saunter up to and serve themselves, and will enjoy whether they are drinking a whisky and soda, a lager, or a glass of Bordeaux. You want dips and spreads.

What follows is a small group of the most mouth-watering and effective dips and spreads. (The quantities given for each will serve about six people without sating them.) I've successfully tried them at pub parties, which of course are the height of informality – though deliciousness and quality count all the more in the circumstances. So, could one ask for less when entertaining at home?

WITH TORTILLA CHIPS OR CRISP PITTA: GUACAMOLE

For the guacamole:
1 large tomato, about 225g/8oz
½ onion
¼ teaspoon salt
2 ripe avocados green or black skinned ,
½ handful coriander, hand chopped
¾ teaspoon, or less, crushed dried chilli

This is really delicious if done properly. My recipe is adapted from Diana Kennedy's authoritative *The Cuisines of Mexico*[13] and avoids what she calls 'the unnecessary additions that I see in most pedestrian cookbooks'. For the crisp dipping bits, fried taco shells or tortilla chips are completely authentic, but avoid using manufactured tortilla chips that come already flavoured with chillis so they can be eaten as self-contained snacks: the spiciness will overwhelm the taste of proper guacamole, which is serenely mild. If you can't buy plain unspiced tortilla chips, I recommend using pitta bread split in half through the centre and lightly toasted, then chopped into tortilla chip-sized pieces.

Nothing will stop this mixture from darkening once it is made, and that looks unappetizing, so it needs to be made shortly before being eaten. Pour boiling water over the tomato, allow it to sit for two minutes, then pour off the water and peel off the loose skin. Quarter the tomato and discard the seeds, then put it in the bowl of a food processor with the half onion, salt, and the skinned and stoned avocados. Whizz to a fine purée, then unclip the bowl and remove the blade. Add the coriander, plus just enough chilli to be definitely there but well in the background: heavily chillied guacamole is incorrect and not as good. Stir the coriander and chilli through manually and put the guacamole in a serving bowl.

---

13 New York, 1972.

WITH TORTILLA CHIPS OR CRISP PITTA: TAPÉNADE

For the tapénade:
100g/3½fl oz capers
150g/5oz anchovies
200g/7oz tinned tuna, drained
55ml/2fl oz lemon juice
About 110ml/3½fl oz olive oil
Ground black pepper
150g/5oz stoned black olives, finely chopped

This is a Provençal caper sauce I've adapted to become a dip in exactly the same fashion as the guacamole in the previous recipe. Inauthentic, but good. As with the guacamole, use unspicy tortilla crisps or split toasted pitta crisps as dipping materials.

Combine the capers, anchovies, tuna and lemon juice in a blender or food processor and blend thoroughly, adding enough oil to make the mixture a little thicker than single cream. Finally add the pepper and stir in the chopped olives by hand, and put the tapénade in a serving bowl.

WITH PITTA BREAD OR SESAME BISCUITS: TARAMÁSALATA

For the taramásalata:
3-6 slices white bread without crusts
165g/6oz Greek taramá or (second choice) English smoked cod's roe
3 garlic cloves
4 tablespoons lemon juice
110ml/3½fl oz olive oil
110ml/3½fl oz cold water
Ground black pepper

Don't buy commercial taramásalata. And unless you can get hold of proper Greek taramá, that is dried salted smoked cod's roe (carp's roe is used in a Middle Eastern version), it may be better to forget this, though an adaptation can be made with the smokier English roe. The Greek stuff is often available in continental groceries and can be found in tins at ambitious supermarkets. If you *can* find it there's nothing better with a drink than taramásalata, a dip for which pitta bread was actually intended. Sesame seed biscuits are also fine.

Wet three slices of the bread and squeeze out, reserving other slices in case the taste of the mixture needs to be made milder. Put the roe, three bread slices and other ingredients including cold water in a food processor and process thoroughly. Taste, and if necessary add more damp bread and some pepper. Put in a serving bowl and serve with slices of pitta bread or sesame biscuits.

ON LARGE BREAD TOASTS: ANCHOÏADE AND PISSALADIÈRE

For the bread base:
6 large hand-cut thick pieces of excellent white bread with plenty of crust, such as 3 ciabattas cut in half the long way, or pieces of focaccia bread

For the anchoïade:
165g/6oz salted anchovies (in oil or not)
6 sun-dried tomatoes (if they are really dry, not sold in oil, then steam them first as a reconstitution)
6 garlic cloves
1 teaspoon lemon juice
20 leaves basil, or 1½ tablespoons dried basil
Enough extra virgin olive oil to make an oily spread

For the pissaladière:
750-900g/27oz-2lb red or yellow sweet onions, thinly sliced
110ml/3½fl oz extra virgin olive oil
55g/2oz stoned black Niçoise olives, oil-cured by preference, chopped
6 garlic cloves, finely chopped (optional)
Salt
6-12 anchovy fillets, as garnish

These are Provençal open-faced sandwich-type snacks. They have crossed the horizon of English cultural awareness in the last ten years, but don't let their newfound popularity spoil them for you – they were born to be fed to guests. Anchoïade is made with an anchovy and tomato mixture, pissaladière is prepared from an oil-stewed onion mixture, and they have equal gastronomic attractions. You could make either on a base of pizza dough or rolled-out bread dough, as is authentically done in Marseilles and Toulon, but it's easier to make them on baked bread, as follows.

Either recipe here requires the quantity of bread given as the base, so if you are doing both, double the amount of bread.

For the anchoïade, reserve a few fillets of anchovy for garnish, then process all the ingredients (if the basil leaves are fresh, leave them out and chop them by hand) in a blender bowl or small food processor with enough oil to make a paste slightly thicker than single cream. Toast the bread slices on the crust side in a very hot oven or under the grill, then spread the anchoïade on the other sides and toast that for 10 more minutes. Garnish with the reserved anchovies before serving hot.

For the pissaladière, put the onions in a frying pan with the oil and sauté them over the lowest possible heat for the longest possible time, with the intention of making them very soft but not brown. Toast the bread slices on the crust side in a very hot oven or under the grill, then spread the onion purée on the other side with a good sprinkling of chopped olives (the garlic as well if using it), and salt if necessary. Toast the onion side for 10 more minutes before serving hot, with anchovy fillets as garnish.

HOT DIP WITH RAW VEGETABLES: BAGNA CAUDA

For the bagna cauda:
165ml/6fl oz olive oil
55g/2oz butter
5 garlic cloves, finely chopped
55g/2oz anchovy fillets, chopped
Salt if necessary
1 small white truffle, fresh or
    tinned, finely chopped
    (optional)

Suggested vegetables in order of preference. All are raw, cut into bite sizes, soaked in ice water shortly before serving and drained:
    Cardoon hearts (which are traditional), if you can find them
    Fennel, cut into sticks
    Young asparagus with tough ends trimmed off
    Cauliflower florets
    Broccoli florets
    Spring onions, trimmed
    Courgettes, cut into sticks
    Carrots, cut into sticks

This Italian peasant dish is a hot anchovy and garlic dip for raw vegetables, and bread is good in it, too. It's a classic snack to be had along with wine but it's equally good with real ale or lager. You need to serve it in one of those earthenware fondue pan thingies over a candle, because it has to stay warm the entire time.

Heat the oil and butter over medium heat in a sauté pan. Add the garlic and sauté it for just a few seconds, then add the anchovies and reduce the heat to the barest simmer. Cook for about 15 minutes until the anchovies become a suspended paste, stirring frequently. Add salt if necessary and the garlic if you are including it towards the end of the cooking. To serve, put the bagna cauda into the fondue pan over the lit warming candle, surrounded by the raw vegetables and some crusty fingers of bread.

COLD DIP WITH RAW VEGETABLES: DILL, SOUR CREAM AND SALMON ROE

For the dill, sour cream and salmon roe dip:
450ml/16fl oz sour cream
½ teaspoon lemon juice
½ handful fresh dill, finely chopped
1½ tablespoons spring onion, finely chopped
1 tablespoon parsley, finely chopped
Pinch of cayenne pepper
225g/8oz salmon roe

Suggested vegetables:
Cucumber, peeled and cut into strips
Celery sticks
Plus other vegetable suggestions under bagna cauda, page 123 (optional)

This ethnically unidentified but rather Scandinavian-style dip is adapted from *Recipes: Wines and Spirits* (editor uncredited), a book published in the Time-Life 'Foods of the World' series, 1968. It's a delicious accompaniment for raw vegetables, and a total contrast to bagna cauda. The greater quantity is because unlike the former, which will coat vegetables thinly, this dip will be scooped up abundantly by guests.

Mix together all ingredients of the dip with a plastic spatula, folding in the salmon roe so as not to crush the eggs. Put in a bowl and refrigerate for at least two hours before serving with the raw vegetables.

5 FOR THE PUBGOING VEGETARIAN

The Mews Pub

THE PLOUGHMAN'S LUNCH AND ONION MARMALADE

One a single plate, with a knife:
1 large piece[15] of unsliced coarse grainy bread hacked off a loaf, or 5 or 6 sugar-free Scottish oatcake biscuits, such as Paterson's (containing oatmeal, vegetable oil, salt and malt extract)
Butter
2 cheeses in thick wedges, preferably Farmhouse (real) Cheddar and another English hard cheese, such as Red Leicester[16]
2 tablespoons Branston pickle (commercial preparation), or mango chutney, or homemade onion marmalade (see below)

'Ploughman's lunch' is a name like toad-in-the-hole, spotted dick or sunny-side up. You have to know the standard ingredients because the name doesn't tell you. According to the British film of the same name, 'the ploughman's lunch' was a calculated bit of ersatz nostalgia made up by public relations people in the 1960s, and I believe it – probably along with the odious designation sometimes given to my entire subject, 'pub grub'. When I ran The Unicorn I was frequently asked for a ploughman's lunch, but because there are so few ploughmen in St James's I hated responding to that. Snotty as I was then, I made people ask for bread and cheese.

The usual unprepossessing ingredients are bread, butter, cheese and what the English call 'pickle', never a Jewish or Polish pickled cucumber, but a brown vinegary sauce of roughly chopped vegetables known in its commercial form as Branston pickle. If you haven't tried it you may wonder, how does Branston pickle taste with cheese? Well, bearing in mind that wine purists say one should drink port with cheese because cheese masks the flavour of a decent wine, Branston pickle certainly gives cheese no quarter, an argument in its favour.[14] If you aspire to gastronomic heights greater than bottled sauce, serve the bread and cheese with Onion Marmalade (the recipe follows). Nowadays I usually serve the cheese with mango chutney, and Scottish oatcakes instead of bread.

If you prefer to stick with tradition, use coarse, grainy, thickly sliced bread. Don't serve the butter in little foil packets unless

---

14 According to the ingredients list on Crosse & Blackwell Branston Pickle, 'The Original and Best', the contents are vegetables in variable proportion (carrots, cauliflower, gherkins, marrows, onions, rutabaga, tomatoes), sugar, vinegar, dates, salt, apple, modified starch, lemon juice, colour (caramel), spices, acetic acid, garlic extract. Crosse & Blackwell is now a division of Nestlé S A of Switzerland! Look homeward, stranger.

15 Without knowing the size or type of your loaf, I can only say that a *generous* piece of bread ought to be nearly one litre in volume.

16 Animal rennet is generally used in the cheeses I'm recommending. To suit strict vegetarians, substitute cheeses made from vegetable rennets.

you insist on a mimesis of pubstyle. Two cheeses are nicer than one. Of course Cheddar (unlike Champagne) has lost its birthright and can be nearly anything coming from anywhere, but in Britain the term 'Farmhouse Cheddar' denotes a non-factory-made Cheddar from the actual Cheddar Gorge or nearby, and it doesn't cost a fortune. This is what I serve in a thick wedge, always leaving on the bit of cheesecloth-marked rind for beauty and authenticity. My second selection is Red Leicester or another somewhat differently-coloured hard cheese. Most of the great English cheeses are hard. Stilton is unheard of for a ploughman's lunch.

Bread/oatcakes, cheese, and a pint of real ale makes a satisfying working lunch, and the customer doesn't return to the afternoon battles inebriated.

ONION MARMALADE

900g/2lb onions, thinly sliced
110g/4oz butter
2 tablespoons granulated sugar
75ml/3fl oz sherry vinegar, or red wine vinegar
2 tablespoons Grenadine syrup
Salt and a lot of ground black pepper
½ bottle red wine

Super-luxurious for ploughman's lunch, this also makes a perfect accompaniment to meats such as sliced cold terrine, cooked chops or roasted gamefowl. My recipe is the French bourgeois cooking standard, the only main change due to the fact that I find their 'jam' too sweet for a drinker's palate and have reduced the sugar. Put up in large quantities and bottled in handsome jars, this can be a reputation-maker.

Sizzle the onions with the butter in a sauté pan. Add sugar, salt and pepper. Lower the heat and cover, simmering for 20 minutes with an occasional stir. Then add vinegar, Grenadine syrup (always found on a pub's backbar, though not much used since the days of Tequila Mockingbirds – Crème de Cassis can be substituted), and red wine. Cook, uncovered, over low heat with more stirring as necessary until the sauce thickens and bubbles slowly.

LEEKS VINAIGRETTE

900g/2lb leeks if young, thin and tender; buy 1.3kg/3lb if they seem old, fat and tough

For the vinaigrette:
110ml/3½fl oz groundnut oil or other taste-free vegetable oil
55ml/2fl oz white wine vinegar
3 tablespoons Dijon mustard
1 teaspoon brown sugar
Salt and ground black pepper

For a vegetarian person, this cold dish is an excellent starter. For a beefatarian, porkatarian or other fleshatarian, not to mention Rotarian, this underrated dish goes well with a plate of cold cuts. Local leeks reach the market in autumn and winter, with the new slender leeks finding us in early October. You should choose the thinnest ones in the market because you have to discard too much of them if they are large and coarse.

Chop off the leeks' stem and leaf ends, and tear off most of the dark green outer leaves. Discard them, or save for making stock. The only parts wanted are the white slim centres, about 18-23cm/7-9in long. To clean them, slit the leeks lengthwise no more than halfway through, almost to the bottom. Fan them out and rinse them under the tap, but keep them together as cylinders of leaves. Blanch the leek cylinders in boiling, salted water for about 3 minutes, then drain them in a colander for at least an hour.

Shake up the vinaigrette in a jar – it should look thick, yellow and opaque. Immerse the leek cylinders in the vinaigrette for at least an hour before serving.

LASAGNE CON LE VERDURE, OR VEGETABLE LASAGNE

For the vegetables (ingredients may vary; these are typical):
2 medium onions, chopped about 1.5cm/⅝in thick
4 courgettes, sliced about 1.5cm/⅝in thick
2 red capsicum peppers *with* skin, stems removed, seeded and sliced in about 5cm/2in pieces
½ small pumpkin *with* skin, seeded and sliced in about 5cm/2in pieces
1 head garlic, cloves separated but unpeeled and unsliced
Chervil and tarragon or other available fresh herbs, in reasonably plentiful quantity, chopped
Salt and ground black pepper
3 tablespoons olive oil

For the bechamel sauce:
1 500ml/18fl oz container prepared Chef Béchamel – or from the ingredients on page 56
250ml/9fl oz vegetable stock, (fresh, or made with a red pepper stock cube if available, or else from any vegetable stock cube)

For the pasta:
340g/12oz commercial fresh lasagne pasta, or homemade from ingredients – see page 56
Vegetable oil to grease baking tin
Fresh herbs, chopped, as garnish

It's unfortunate that what's universally thought of as lasagne contains meat ragú (see page 56 for the latter). If meat lasagne had never been born or it had a different name, then lasagne con le verdure, this all-vegetable version, would probably get the great recognition it deserves. It's wonderfully good and by no means only to be appreciated by vegetarians. I do it in a rather revisionist way because *I first roast the vegetables.*

When you decide to make it, your choice of vegetables should be seasonal ones; my ingredients are a typical autumn selection. If available, an important constituent is the pulpy texture of pumpkin or squash. Since my pre-baked vegetables become browned and almost caramelised, the usual addition of Parmesan cheese is unnecessary, so this is a fairly healthy recipe in cardio-vascular terms (well, there is that cream in the béchamel which may also obviate this dish for vegans).

I generally use prepared Chef Bechamel, a product made by the Italian company Parmalat; see the introduction to meat lasagne on page 56 for further details. As for the pasta, the broad lasagne pasta layers must either be made freshly at home, or bought as 'fresh lasagne pasta' in an Italian grocery or good supermarket. This dish can't be done well with dry packaged pasta.

One final comment. I don't accept as a general notion that good cooking can be reduced to a few tricks or secrets, but this dish has three that make it wonderful rather than ordinary: do roast the vegetables first, don't blanch the pasta first, don't mix through the béchamel sauce – just pour it on top.

Pre-roast the vegetables by putting them all with the garlic, herbs and seasoning in a roasting pan, tucking the fresh herbs under the heavier vegetable so they don't burn. Drizzle oil over. Roast at your oven's highest heat for up to 1 hour, removing when the top vegetables are pretty blackened but not burned to a crisp.

Meanwhile, either make your fresh béchamel sauce according to instructions on page 57, or warm up your readymade Chef Bechamel. Mix in the stock.

A rectangular baking tin is orthodox for lasagne, but I prefer a round one to make a lasagne for four. Don't blanch the pasta first. Grease the tin with vegetable oil, then layer the sheets of pasta and roasted vegetables alternately, starting and ending with pasta – for a *minceur* version, three pasta layers, for a *gourmande* version, four. Finally, pour béchamel sauce on top in a nonchalant manner and let it find its own way down (don't enthusiastically saturate every level with béchamel or the lasagne will be soggy – you may decide you don't need the entire quantity).

Correct the seasoning if necessary, sprinkle chopped fresh herbs on top and bake for 45 minutes at 150°C/300°F/Gas 2. When out of the oven, cool the lasagne for a few moments so the outer sauce hardens, then slice into pie wedges and serve alongside some uncooked sprigs of fresh herbs such as coriander or flat-leaf parsley.

MACARONI CHEESE

500g/18oz dried macaroni
2 eggs, beaten
170ml/6fl oz milk
1 teaspoon dry mustard
Salt
Paprika
340g/12oz Cheddar cheese, shredded
45g/1½oz breadcrumbs
30g/1oz butter

As with Tuna Noodle Salad (page 81), don't fool around with fresh pasta for this – you need to start with a packet of dried macaroni, as in the old days before fresh pasta arrived. If you don't have to serve this as a vegetarian dish it goes well with a few slices of baked ham. But it's perfectly fine on its own, as generations who have had it at school dinners will attest.

Cook the macaroni for a bit less time than that specified on the packet, then drain.

Butter a baking dish or casserole and put in layers of macaroni, the eggs and milk and seasonings mixed together, and cheese, ending with cheese. Heat the breadcrumbs in a pan with butter and put them on top. Bake in a 175°C/350°F/Gas 4 oven for about half an hour, or until the top becomes golden brown.

NOODLE BAKE WITH ROAST VEGETABLES

750g/27oz noodles (for type, see introduction)
340ml/12fl oz milk
4 or 5 eggs, separated
15g/½oz butter, melted
1 teaspoon salt
½ teaspoon Tabasco sauce or crushed dried chilli
Nutmeg, freshly ground
Butter
Parmesan cheese, freshly grated

This begins with a pan-made version of noodle ring, an American homespun classic used as a crisp accompaniment for anything a bit squishy like creamed chicken or creamed salmon (ugh). The American food expert James Beard says: 'a noodle ring was for many years considered a most sophisticated base for various made dishes. While it is still occasionally found here and there, it is more of a novelty now than a regular.'

In America the gooey main part of the dish, usually eked out with a bit of rice, would be served up within the hollow centre of the noodle ring, all ready for the *Good Housekeeping* photographer or for the 1950s family to cry out with delight. Since baked noodle has never become well known in Britain, it seems stunningly original as an alternative to sautéed potatoes or chips if served with breast of chicken. It also makes a fine vegetarian dish with roasted vegetables.

As for ingredients, in the States one can buy packets that are simply labelled 'noodles', but in the European Union we usually need to buy our pasta by Italian name. The standard one for this dish is tagliatelle, but fettucine is also fine. The wide and deckle-edged pappardelle might be a bodacious choice.

As the noodles will cook a lot afterwards and they mustn't end up very soft, only parboil them to begin with and drain. They should be a few minutes short of al dente. Beat together milk, egg yolks and melted butter, then combine with the noodles. Season with salt, Tabasco and nutmeg. Beat the egg whites until they hold their peaks but are not dry, and fold into the noodle mixture.

For the roast vegetables
(ingredients may vary; those
below are typical):
2 onions, chopped about
1.5cm/⅝in thick
4 courgettes or 1 aubergine,
sliced about 1.5cm/⅝in thick
2 red peppers *with* skin, stems
removed, seeded and sliced
about 1.5cm/⅝in thick
½ small pumpkin *with* skin,
seeded and sliced about
1.5cm/⅝in thick
1 head garlic, cloves separated
but unpeeled and unsliced
Thyme, basil, oregano, chervil,
tarragon or other fresh herbs,
in reasonably plentiful
quantity, chopped
2 tablespoons olive oil
Salt and ground black pepper

Pour into a well-buttered baking pan of a size so the noodles are at least 2.5cm/1in and not more than 5cm/2in deep. Bake at 175°C/350°F/Gas 4 for 45-50 minutes, or until the eggs have set and the tops of the noodles are browned. (You may find that a minute or two under the grill afterwards is required to produce the ideal golden brown/hard crust, atop the custardy interior, around ribbons that retain their own third texture.) Finally, sprinkle while hot with a bit of freshly grated Parmesan cheese. Cut through the tough crust with a sharp knife and serve in 7.5cm/3in squares.

For the roast vegetables, put the vegetables, garlic, herbs and seasoning in a roasting pan with the delicate herbs underneath some of the chunkier vegetables so they don't burn. Drizzle oil over, and roast at highest oven heat for about an hour. The vegetables on top will get blackened but they shouldn't be burnt to a crisp.

PENNE (WITH BROCCOLI) IN GARLIC SAUCE

800g/30oz fresh Italian penne pasta (small tubes with quill-like ends)
400g/14oz broccoli, cut into 2.5cm/1in sprays (optional)

For the garlic sauce:
6 large garlic cloves, peeled
6-8 sundried tomatoes
4 anchovy fillets in oil (optional but desirable)
½ teaspoon salt
½ teaspoon ground pepper
½ teaspoon crushed dried chilli
55-75ml/2-2½fl oz extra virgin olive oil
10-15 fresh basil leaves, or 3 teaspoons dried basil
20-30 fresh oregano leaves, or 3 teaspoons dried oregano
110g/4oz Parmesan cheese, freshly grated on medium holes of grater

One of the great challenges of pub cooking is to achieve a delicious, satisfying, simple-to-prepare pasta dish. It would be eternally popular and it could be perennially on offer on the menu blackboard. To accomplish this in vegetarian form, and in a way that doesn't require cooking (apart from the pasta) would be astonishing – and that's almost my claim for this dish. 'Almost', because there are two cavils: in its best-tasting version the sauce includes some anchovy which invalidates it for serious vegetarians. And it has such a lot of garlic in it that customers must be warned, which I do with its name.

Oddly, this dish evolved through my husband's need to diet. After a long struggle with indifferent results, his doctor suggested lunchtime dishes of pasta to feel replete and keep from snacking. Nathan found this revolutionary concept worked brilliantly as long as the calories in the dish were due mainly to the pasta, with scant animal protein and fat added. Since he worked at home where he could garlic up a storm, he experimented for months with pasta sauces, chiefly aided by a Braun hand blender with separate plastic beaker and chopper. (This device is invaluable for making small quantities of processed ingredients, but other chopping methods do almost as well, and for four people – as below – one may as well use a food processor.)

At my pub if someone planning a private party asks for a dish that would suit vegetarians, I may suggest penne and broccoli with the sauce below, *sans* anchovy. As normally prepared for the pub menu, the anchovies are included.

For the pasta and broccoli, boil water in two pans. Penne generally requires 5 or 6 minutes to become al dente; broccoli requires 10 or 12 minutes until it becomes barely tender.

While cooking, combine the ingredients for the garlic sauce, except for the fresh herb leaves and cheese, and blend together in the food processor. Either add the fresh leaves to the processor at the end for a very quick additional chop, or chop the leaves by hand and stir them into the sauce.

Drain the penne and broccoli and toss them together in a large bowl with the sauce and the grated Parmesan.

FOCACCIA BREAD WITH TOMATO, GARLIC AND PINE NUTS, AND OTHER FOCACCIA VARIATIONS

1 tin (400g/14oz) chopped
    tomatoes
4 pieces focaccia bread, each
    about 15 x 15cm/6 x 6in
6 garlic cloves, very finely
    chopped
12 anchovy fillets
75ml/3fl oz extra virgin olive oil
3 tablespoons pine nuts

Focaccia bread is available at large supermarkets. In London it can certainly be found at Camisa in Old Compton Street, and probably at a number of other Italian grocers – ask around. What is it? It's a large flat leavened loaf perhaps 7.5 x7.5 x3cm/3 x 3 x 1in. In other words, a sort of big square pizza, except that it's made with bread dough rather than pizza (durum semolina) dough. At Camisa it's sold in cut sections or pieces.

The great thing is that focaccia can be used as a base for all sorts of grilled or baked pizza-type toppings, vegetarian or not. In addition to the one suggested in the recipe, it's perfect for topping with anchoïade or pissaladière (page 122), or with something like finely sliced grilled aubergine sprinkled with olive oil and pine nuts on top of a crumbled mild sheep's milk cheese, or maybe plain skinned red pepper strips sprinkled with olive oil, blackened in a very hot oven, and garnished with chopped coriander. These and other variations can all be dealt with by roasting as described below.

Spread the chopped tomato on the four pieces of focaccia, then on top of that place a neatly distributed arrangement of the fine garlic and anchovy fillets. Drizzle with olive oil and scatter on the pine nuts. Bake in a 230°C/450°F/Gas 8 oven for about 25 minutes, or until the tomato has darkened and the pine nuts have started to blacken.

6

DRINKS FROM THE THREE GREYHOUNDS AND PARTIES AT HOME

The Jug and Bottle at the
Green Man

A GOOD BLOODY MARY

In a highball or Slim Jim glass:
A moderate amount of crushed ice
3 measures vodka, preferably containing chillis
Nearly fill with tomato juice
3 dashes Worcestershire sauce
(1 dash Tabasco sauce if plain vodka is used)
1 dash lemon juice
½ teaspoon celery seeds (N.B. important secret ingredient)
Pinch of salt

It's a well-known phrase, you know: 'I need a good Bloody Mary'. So though pubs seldom bother to make them well, here's how. (I prepare the vodka containing chillis myself by putting long red chillis in a large bottle of vodka and displaying it on the back bar.)

Give it a good stir. Serve ideally, with a thin stick of celery swizzle, or as second choice, a slice of lemon.

A PERFECT DRY MARTINI

In a wide conical 110ml/3½fl oz cocktail glass:
90ml/3¼fl oz frozen high proof (40% vol.) Beefeater or Tanqueray gin
5ml/⅛ fl oz (that's 1 teaspoon maximum!) Noilly Prat
2 pearl onions

'Why is a Dry Martini like a woman's breasts? Because one is not enough, and three are too many'. It's a sexist joke, but it happens to be true. Provided each one delivers 110ml/3½fl oz of undiluted cocktail.

What makes mine perfect are (1) high-proof excellent gin, such as Beefeater or Tanqueray (and *never* vodka), (2) subtly fragrant Noilly Prat extra-dry vermouth (preferable to the Martini brand the cocktail was named for), (3) no melted ice to dilute the drink because the gin is kept in the freezer, (4) a 110ml/3½fl oz cocktail glass. My strong preference is for a garnish of two pearl onions rather than one pimento olive, which technically makes it a Gibson, but so what: I still call it a dry martini.

Use no ice. And there's neither shaking *nor* stirring. The aroma of fine vermouth floats to the top; dropping in the onions is all the agitation it needs.

EGGNOG, NASHVILLE STYLE

2 bottles bourbon
1 bottle dark Jamaican rum
1 bottle Cognac
700g/25oz sugar
20 cloves
28 eggs
4 litres/7 pints single cream
Nutmeg (ready-ground is less
　　flavourful, but easier)

This American recipe for a Victorian English classic (I think that must have been its origin) makes a marvellous punch for Christmas, or for a wedding party – I made it for mine – because it contains the liquid equivalent of a rich cake plus copious alcohol. The only problems are that drinkers won't want much to eat after having three cups of it, and you ought to have a conscience about serving so much cholesterol if the guests will be older than about 35 to 40. The bottles indicated are the regular 70cl size. Serves about 50.

On Christmas Eve or the day before the wedding, mix the bourbon, rum, Cognac, sugar and cloves in a punchbowl or clean bucket, and allow to stand for 6 hours. Next, separate the eggs, then add the beaten yolks to the booze a little at a time. Cover the punchbowl with either a lid or a plastic carrier bag tied with string to restrict evaporation of alcohol, and allow to stand overnight. Make sure the cream will be very cold on the morrow.

A few hours before the party next day, whip the egg whites until stiff. Add the cream and egg whites separately to the booze mixture, a little at a time, folding in the egg whites. Sprinkle with plenty of nutmeg before serving. This is delicious frozen, so freeze a little for dessert after the guests leave.

A FOGGY DAY

Ingredients: see text

When *Crazy for You* opened in London a few years ago at the Prince Edward Theatre across the street from The Three Greyhounds, I decided to honour the Gershwin-London relationship with a new cocktail. Here's what the press release said:

The combination of London, a new musical by the Gershwins based on an old one from 1930, and the age of cocktails (the '20s and '30s), have all come together at The Three Greyhounds, across the street from the Prince Edward Theatre, where publican Roxy Beaujolais has created a new cocktail to honour *Crazy For You.*

A FOGGY DAY is a unique evocation of its various inspirations. As its ingredients include London gin and ginger beer, they are truly British. Moreover, viewed sideways in the glass, they are reassuringly foggy. The cocktail uses a garnish of Hong Kong candied stem ginger that looks the colour of London brick. Is even more symbolism necessary? The slices of ginger are impaled on a blue cocktail stick which may remind drinkers that, according to Mr Ira Gershwin, 'the outlook was decidedly blue'. (That outlook continued until Fred Astaire, playing an American in London in the 1937 Gershwin film *A Damsel In Distress* for which the song was written, 'suddenly . . . saw you there'. 'You' was Joan Fontaine.)

But *you* can be there now, at the launch of the new cocktail, attended by members of the cast of *Crazy For You* and authentic jazz age musicians: 11am, 6 April 1993, The Three Greyhounds, corner of Greek Street at Old Compton Street.

For those who wish to try this strangely delicious new cocktail at home, here is the recipe:

In a chilled conical cocktail glass with its rim dipped in white sugar, add:

2 measures London gin in a bottle from the freezer

2 measures chilled high-quality ginger beer

Small slices of candied stem ginger on a blue cocktail stick. (Gin, ginger beer, ginger – all Gs, for Gershwin and Greyhounds, geddit?)

So now the world knows how to make it – as invented by Roxy Beaujolais at The Three Greyhounds, where it can be always be drunk within sight of *Crazy For You*!

It's delicious but, you may ask, is it really original? We checked *The Esquire Drink Book*, an encyclopaedic cocktail compendium from the old days. This has recipes for 227 mixed drinks with a gin base, and only one of those gin cocktails includes ginger as a mentioned ingredient. Strangely enough it is called a London Buck, made from gin and the juice of half a lemon, served over cracked ice and topped with American ginger ale. It isn't very impressive. (OK, a Moscow Mule is also made with ginger beer, but as its name suggests it has a vodka base and lime juice.) As the press release concluded:

If you 'view the morning with alarm', we advise you to try A FOGGY DAY. The sun will be 'shining ev'rywhere!'

A STIFF ONE

3 parts Irish Mist or Drambuie
3 parts vodka
3 parts lemon juice
2 parts Cointreau or Triple Sec
1 part Grenadine

The impact of an alcoholic drink is proportional to the amount of its alcohol, or so it's widely believed. Strangely, though, experimentation reveals this isn't consistently true. Certain flavour esters, liquids or substances seem to combine with alcohol causing increased body absorption. The alcohol gets moving through the system very fast. Though its amount might have been judged reasonable, a breathalyser – which, measuring alcoholic throughput, makes a fair assessment – would go bananas.

I mention this because when planning a party for the staff and guests of a coroner's court, we realised we would be hosts to members of the legal profession sadly in need of bucking up. In homage, we set out to invent a cocktail called A Stiff One, and we thought the name ought to ring rather true. Our researches led us to an infamous '30s drink called a Blowtorch, because legend had it that bartenders were surprised if anyone could pronounce the name to ask for a second. It is a mixture of Southern Comfort, gin, Triple Sec, orange juice and Grenadine, and we found that despite ⅓ths of the Blowtorch being juice, it made us forget many sorrows.

So all that was needed was a reasonable modification to make the drink our own. This we hoped to achieve by replacing the Southern Comfort with Irish Mist or Drambuie. Then we tasted it. No. Too sweet. Substitute lemon juice for the orange juice. Reduce the Cointreau. What was the gin supposed to be doing? We couldn't tell. Substitute vodka for the gin. At last it was perfect – delicious, yet dynamic. You see how scientists do their research? And I'm proud to say that the British Isles origin of our own sweet liqueur alternative seems to work no less effectively with the other ingredients in making the alcohol set off screaming round one's system.

Agitate all ingredients with cracked ice or cubes, strain, and pour into a stemmed cocktail glass without garnish.

BIBLIOGRAPHY OF BOOKS ABOUT PUBS

Batchelor, Denzil: THE ENGLISH INN (London 1963)

Bickerdyke, John: THE CURIOSITIES OF ALE & BEER: An Entertaining History (London 1889)

Burke, Thomas, ed.: THE BOOK OF THE INN (London 1927)

Burke, Thomas: THE ENGLISH INN (London 1931)

Case, Frank: TALES OF A WAYWARD INN [The Algonquin Hotel, New York] (New York 1939)

Fothergill, John: AN INNKEEPER'S DIARY (London 1931)

Girouard, Mark: THE VICTORIAN PUB (New Haven 1975)

Gorham, Maurice: BACK TO THE LOCAL (London 1949)

Gorham, Maurice: INSIDE THE PUB (London 1950)

Hindley, Charles: TAVERN ANECDOTES AND SAYINGS; Including the Origin of Signs, and Reminiscences Connected With Taverns, Coffee-Houses, Clubs, Etc Etc (London 1875)

Keverne, Richard: TALES OF OLD INNS (London 1939)

Mabey, David, ed.: THE WHICH? GUIDE TO COUNTRY PUBS (London 1993)

McGill, Angus, ed.: 1996 EVENING STANDARD LONDON PUB GUIDE (London 1995)

Monckton, Herbert A: A HISTORY OF THE ENGLISH PUBLIC HOUSE (London 1969)

Ogden, Archibald G: LONDON FOR EVERYONE (New York 1966)

Selley, Ernest: THE ENGLISH PUBLIC HOUSE AS IT IS (London 1927)

Spiller, Brian: VICTORIAN PUBLIC HOUSES (Newton Abbot 1972)

1996 TIME OUT GUIDE TO EATING AND DRINKING IN LONDON (London 1995)

1996 TIME OUT LONDON GUIDE (London 1995)

Wagner, Leopold: LONDON INNS AND TAVERNS (London 1924)

Whitbread and Co Ltd: THE BREWER'S ART (London 1948)

Whitbread and Co Ltd: WORD FOR WORD: An Encyclopædia of Beer (London 1953)

INDEX